Mary Helen —

Joy to you
in every precious
moment!

Love!
Bric
Burr

W9-BYJ-667

BEYOND SUCCESS

*The 15 Secrets
of a Winning Life!*

As a young assistant under John Wooden I learned lessons about real success that changed my life. Now, a new master, Brian Biro, builds upon those same **timeless principles to guide you *Beyond Success* so you can win the biggest championship of all—a life of purpose and joy.** A master gameplan for a truly winning life.
   —Denny Crum
   Head Basketball Coach, University of Louisville

Biro's *Beyond Success* reads like the final seconds of a NCAA playoff, only I get to replay it over and over and over again. Just like Coach Wooden, this book is **alive with calculated, confident brilliance.** This is a fast-break play for life!
   —Harvey Mackay
   Author, *Swim With the Sharks Without Being Eaten Alive*

Beyond Success reflects the humility, kindness, and tremendous sense of humor that has characterized the leadership and life of Coach John Wooden, **building upon the foundational principles of a master—this book is great!**
   —Jim Harrick
   Head Basketball Coach, University of California, Los Angeles
   1995 NCAA Championship Title

Beyond Success is one of those rare books that has actually stood up, walked about, spoken, and taken an active role in shaping my life. **Brian Biro is one of those rare teachers who has deeply and permanently altered how I see myself and my world.** Brian and *Beyond Success* have touched me and changed me for the better forever—and I bet they will you, too!
   —John David Mann
   Editor, *Upline™* magazine

Beyond Success is **a fascinating, in-depth study** of Coach John Wooden's leadership techniques. If they work only half as well for you as they worked for Coach Wooden, you and the people you lead will be fabulously successful.

—Dr. Tony Alessandra
Author, *The Art of Managing*

Brian Biro has captured Coach John Wooden's timeless philosophies in *Beyond Success* and woven them into **a timeless leadership formula** that should help us all in every aspect of our lives.

—Ken Blanchard
Co-author, *The One Minute Manager*

Brian Biro's book eloquently captures the spirit of the Pyramid of Success that has been as synonymous with Coach John Wooden as has been the ten NCAA basketball championships that his Bruin teams won in an extraordinary 12-year span.

While the media attention that accompanied Coach Wooden's stay at the top of the college basketball world made him a familiar figure to all sports fans, **it was and is his Pyramid of Success that truly brings his greatness to everyone regardless of their interest in college sports.**

This book brings to life the real essence of Coach John Wooden and the part of his greatness that has more relevance and more meaning for every reader than the thrill of a victory on the basketball court.

—Charles E. Young
Chancellor, University of California, Los Angeles

In the new world of interdependency, **the 15 Secrets govern.** The proven Wooden leadership tapestry is based on fundamental principles, not cute, cosmetic, cotton candy techniques. Brian Biro weaves this tapestry around absolutely compelling true stories.

—Stephen R. Covey
Author, *The 7 Habits of Highly Effective People*

An interesting and insightful look at **the philosophies of a legend.** Brian Biro is a wonderful communicator.
    —R. M. Geschwind
        President and CEO, Southwestern Bell Yellow Pages

At last, here is a book that marries leadership, management, and teams! Brian Biro has punctuated Coach Wooden's principles with **real life stories to which every leader, manager, and team player can relate.** The business world thanks you!
    —Judy Henrichs
        President, The MatCon Alliance

I found myself underlining so many sentences and starring so many paragraphs that before I was halfway through, **I knew** *Beyond Success* **would take its place beside the few books I consider to be treasures.** If you recognize the value of ideas, you won't put this book down.
    —Daryl Kollman
        CEO and Chairman, Cell Tech

An exciting, stimulating, and practical approach . . . Brian Biro presents **an integrated and supremely effective system for leadership development** that begins where it must—on the personal level.
    —Barry Z. Posner, Ph.D.
        Professor and Managing Partner, Executive Development
        Center, Santa Clara University
        Co-author, *The Leadership Challenge* and *Credibility*

An **inspiring and uplifting guide to personal effectiveness** by an inspiring and uplifting human being. Brian Biro is a leader for our time.
    —John Robbins
        Author, *Diet For A New America* and *May All Be Fed*

Brian Biro has made tangible the intangibles of defining the characteristics of leadership. **One can't read this book and not immediately become a more successful participant in all areas of life**—and, more important, a better human being. It's a great book.

—Roger Staubach
Pro Football Hall of Fame
CEO, The Staubach Company

Brian Biro's book brings to life the timeless philosophies of John Wooden—something all of us need to focus on. I have been blessed to know Coach Wooden for twenty-five years. This fine book **allows everyone else the privilege of learning how to apply a true genius' way of life to their everyday experiences.** A terrific read from a hard working author.

—Bill Walton
NCAA and Naismith Memorial Basketball Halls of Fame
Commentator, CBS Sports

Thank you Brian for sharing with me your 15 Secrets, which I can use to enrich my life and the lives of people around me. Your service-oriented spirit flows through each insightful secret. **You have inspired me to move out of my comfort zone to work harder to serve those around me better.** I look forward to experiencing some new adventures in life as I practice your secrets. Everyone should put *Beyond Success* on their must-read list.

—Glen Davidson
President, Concord Communications, Inc.

Great stories from great champions . . . The watchword for the 21st century is building championship *teams,* and Brian's model of the Wooden Blocks is what I have chosen to follow.

—Jan Ruhe
Author, *Pour Yourself a Cup of Ambition*
Editor-in-Chief, *PowerNews*
Diamond Sales Director, Discovery Toys

On life's balance sheet, the people who work with you, day in and day out, to create the superior service or product you deliver to your customers are one of your most highly valued assets. No one explains this better than Brian Biro, **a leader of leaders who uncovers the greatness in everyone he touches.** Anyone who cares at all about real success—honoring and advancing the innate talents and unlimited potential of others—must read this book.

   —John McCormack
       CEO, Visible Changes
       Author, *Self-Made in America*

As the next millennium approaches, one key resource is emerging as the critical ingredient needed for each of us to become winners—having a great coach. From sports we know Lombardi, Wooden, Aurbach . . . But what you and I really need is an empowering coach from the playing fields of entrepreneurship and personal productivity . . . **a coach who has the vision, awareness and commitment to have us play full out to achieve our own championship performance.** After reading *Beyond Success*, I have a new coach: Brian Biro.

   —John Milton Fogg
       Editor-in-Chief, Upline™
       Author, *The Greatest Networker in the World*

Brian Biro is **the leader for a new generation** of individuals and organizations who know that the secrets of success lie in what the team creates together.

   —Marta Kollman
       President, Cell Tech

BEYOND SUCCESS

The 15 Secrets of a Winning Life!

BRIAN D. BIRO

Pygmalion Press
Hamilton, Montana

Pygmalion Press
P.O. Box 1130
Hamilton, MT 59840-1130

Copyright ©1995 by Brian D. Biro

All rights reserved. Printed in the United States of America. No part of this publication may be reproduced, stored in a retrieval system or transmitted in any form or by any means, electronic, mechanical, photocopying, recording or otherwise without the written permission of the publisher.

Pygmalion Press books and tapes may be purchased for educational, business or sales promotional use. For information please call or write Special Markets Department, Shinetop Productions, 4067 Santa Nella Place, San Diego, CA 92130, or call (619) 481-6561, or fax (619) 481-6301.

Designed and illustrated in part by Robert Mott & Associates
Edited by Just Write
Illustrated in part by Brian Lemke

The following excerpts are reprinted with permission:

Kareem by Kareem Abdul-Jabbar. Copyright © 1990 by Kareem Abdul-Jabbar. Used by permission of Random House, Inc.

Leadership Is an Art by Max DePree. Copyright © 1987 by Max DePree. Used by permission of Doubleday, a division of Bantam Doubleday Dell Publishing Group, Inc.

Leadership When the Heat's On by Danny Cox. Copyright © 1992 by McGraw-Hill. Used by permission of McGraw-Hill, Inc.

Son Rise: The Miracle Continues by Barry Neil Kaufman. Copyright © 1994 by Barry Neil Kaufman. Used by permission of The Option Institute and Fellowship.

They Call Me Coach by John Wooden with Jack Tobin. Copyright © 1988. Used with permission of Contemporary Books, Inc., Chicago.

Library of Congress Cataloging-in-Publication Data

Biro, Brian D.
    Beyond success : the 15 secrets of a winning life! / Brian D. Biro
        Hamilton, Mont. : Pygmalion Press, 1995.
        xxi, 346 p. : ill. ; 24 cm.
        Includes index.
        ISBN 0-9647453-0-5 (cloth)
            1. Success—Psychological aspects.   2. Character.   3. Leadership—
    Psychological aspects.   I. Title.

    BF637.S8B49   1995   170'.44—dc20   95-78989
                                                                              AACR 2 MARC

Printed in the United States of America

96   97   98   99   \   10   9   8   7   6   5   4   3   2

DEDICATION

*To Carole, Kelsey, and Jenna, who teach me
each day about the single greatest secret
to a winning life—
sharing every precious moment
with those
you love unconditionally.
Thank you for filling my life with love, joy,
and compelling purpose.*

Acknowledgments

When I set out to fulfill my life's dream of writing a book that captured the essence of the immense potential each of us possesses to impact others, I was struck by a very important realization: Although many of us have been deeply affected at some point in our lives by individuals who provided leadership, faith, or support when we needed it most, it is rare for us to fully appreciate these mentors and guides who have illuminated our pathways to understanding. These are our life coaches. Their inspiration and example are so deeply ingrained in our being that we sometimes forget the original source.

Through the stories and ideas you are about to enjoy, I seek to honor and acknowledge the primary catalysts in my life—whose example, energy, and inspiration have helped me to know that there is genius in all of us. You will find that this book offers an unusual and refreshing approach to sharing powerful principles of personal growth and leadership because it is put together like a championship relay team. My great teachers lead off the relay in grand style by sharing their knowledge and foundational principles. Every page is enlivened with the wisdom of these magnificent coaches, some of whom you may already know—giants such as Mahatma Gandhi, Napoleon Hill, John Robbins, Stephen Covey, Anthony Robbins, and Viktor Frankl. You will also meet several others including Daryl and Marta Kollman; Barry

Kaufman; Pablo Morales; Jim Rohn; Elzea Bufiér; Max DePree; my parents, Louis and Miriam Biro; and my closest and most constant teachers—my wife, Carole, and my daughters, Kelsey and Jenna. In *Beyond Success: The 15 Secrets of a Winning Life* I have taken the baton from these great teachers and built upon their timeless wisdom with my own ideas and personal stories. As you apply the fifteen secrets you will find yourself running the anchor leg yourself, accelerating toward your own winning life!

All great relay teams are supported by a master coach. I feel incredibly fortunate to have received the guidance of the very best, Coach John Wooden. His is an example of a truly winning life. He demonstrates the immense possibility available to us when we learn to focus beyond success onto building character and providing leadership for ourselves and others, thus moving ever closer to true personal fulfillment.

John Wooden remains the most acclaimed college basketball coach in the history of the National Collegiate Athletics Association (NCAA). In his final twelve years at UCLA, his teams won a staggering total of ten NCAA Championships. No other coach has won more than four. He is the only individual ever to be elected to the College Basketball Hall of Fame as both a player and a coach. He is truly one of a kind—a genuine legend to whom all others in his field will forever be compared.

Yet it is not *what* Coach Wooden has accomplished that is the measure of his greatness. It is *how* he achieved these legendary results—by exemplifying the very essence of integrity and class. This kind, sincere, and ethical man personifies the leadership qualities that are so desperately needed in our business, political, educational, and family environments today. His contributions to this book and to my life are treasured gifts.

Beyond Success: The 15 Secrets of a Winning Life is a dream transformed into reality. It would not have been possible without the unending support of the superb editing team from Just Write: Karen Risch and Deena Tuttle. I am deeply grateful to these remarkably talented women. I also wish to express my special thanks to Robert Mott and Gail Fink of Robert Mott & Associates, for their caring and top quality graphic design, layout, and production; and to Jonathan Hulsh for his gentle guidance and creative genius. My friends, Raphiella Adamson and Nick Daley, were always there with their generous support to keep this project moving forward.

Finally, I am especially honored to acknowledge my special friend, Larry Michel of Shinetop Productions, for his immeasurable contributions to *Beyond Success.* Larry's inexhaustible energy and undying faith in this book kept the light burning bright at the end of the tunnel, every step of the way.

Contents

Foreword

I have been blessed with a wonderful, fulfilling life. Over my years as a teacher and a coach I have had the honor and privilege of working with thousands of remarkable people. At UCLA we were fortunate enough to win ten NCAA Basketball Championships in the last twelve years I served as coach. This record has yet to be approached.

The championship streak was well earned by the young men who gave their all as dedicated team players. Yet, to truly understand how the record was accomplished, it is important to realize that I coached for more than twenty-five years before my first NCAA Championship team was crowned. Our ultimate success came from following a philosophy that allowed us to feel successful all during those years of struggle before the first championship banner was raised.

We held firm to the belief that success is not determined by the scoreboard, or even by the won/lost record. Instead we saw success as an internal feeling resulting from the self-satisfaction of knowing we'd given our best to become the best of which we were capable. This belief enabled every member of the team, whether a star like Kareem Abdul-Jabbar or a player who rarely made it into the games, to know he was important and was a genuine contributor.

Nearly sixty years ago I began to develop a structure for personal growth based on this belief about real success. As it took shape, the structure became a foundation for my work as a teacher and coach. Though it appears to be a very simple design, the resulting Pyramid of Success took fourteen years of experimentation and adjustment before I felt solid about its completeness and strength as a model for building character, courage, and compassion. Throughout my twenty-seven years at UCLA, not a day went by that the pyramid did not serve as a source of guidance and inspiration for the way I conducted myself both on the basketball floor and with my family. The pyramid became a road map, simplifying the process of staying on track and living according to my values.

Over the years, I have shared the pyramid through my teachings and writings. It has been very satisfying to see the principles make a positive difference for others as they seek to fulfill their potential.

I first met Brian Biro several years ago when he interviewed me at my home in southern California. At the time we met, Brian was the vice president of a major training company, a position in which he focused on leadership and team building. As we talked that day, it became clear that Brian felt as strongly as I do about the value of the pyramid beyond the athletic field. He envisioned the principles making a significant difference in business, education, and the home. He had applied these ideas effectively throughout his career, first as a very successful swimming coach, and later as an executive in the transportation industry. I saw how thoroughly he grasped the connections between these concepts and how committed he was to taking them to a new level.

In his book, *Beyond Success: The 15 Secrets of a Winning Life!* Brian Biro has captured the essence of my Pyramid of Success and the secrets behind each block as it ascends to the apex. He then goes even further, creating a new game plan for lasting leadership and personal fulfillment.

It is my feeling that real success is not the accumulation of material possessions or the attainment of a position of power or prestige. Rather, it is the peace of mind that is attained only by making the effort to do the best you are capable of doing at any task in which you are engaged. When you embrace this fundamental idea— that your success is determined not by what others think but rather by what you know in your own heart—you have the opportunity to make each day your masterpiece. This is the central message of *Beyond Success: The 15 Secrets of a Winning Life!* Brian Biro brings this message to life in a way that is both compelling and spiritually uplifting.

As a boy growing up on an Indiana farm, I learned a great lesson from my father: Never compare yourself to others. By understanding this principle I was able to feel successful at times when others saw only defeat, and to increase focus and concentration when others became complacent or self-aggrandizing because they felt victory was assured. Success is not trying to be better than someone else—which may be impossible. Success, instead, involves learning from others and trying to reach your own level of competency. Only you alone can determine whether or not you made your best effort. Never permit yourself to become too involved with things you cannot control, as that will adversely affect the things you can control. In *Beyond Success* Brian teaches us that true success is the result of concentrated focus on character rather than reputation. Character is who you really are; reputation is merely what others think you are.

Brian has uncovered new secrets within each block of the pyramid by using captivating and inspiring analogies from his own experience. I was enthralled as he transformed the concept of the pyramid into a complete system of leadership and personal growth that is ideally suited for the demands of an accelerating world. He introduces fresh insights that elevate the applicability and efficacy of the foundational ideas to an exciting new level. As you read his stories and learn about some of the wonderful people he has worked with over the years— like unforgettable little red-haired Allison, the "Thrasher," and Yves LaForest, who scaled mighty Mount Everest— you will begin to develop your own personalized game plan to enrich your life as a parent, a friend, and a professional.

Beyond Success: The 15 Secrets of a Winning Life! makes me feel like a runner in an Olympic relay, having given my very best during my leg of the event and now filled with positive spirit and unlimited support as I hand the baton to my teammate. As you apply the lessons Brian teaches, you will condition yourself mentally, emotionally, morally, and spiritually to run your own leg of the leadership relay to the very best of your ability.

It is my hope that this fine book will be of great and lasting value to people of all ages and walks of life. May it help you find the peace of mind that comes from knowing you have done the best of which you are capable.

John Wooden

Introduction

Remember the 1980s? Baby Boomers who had championed the passionate causes of the sixties and seventies—the antiwar movement, Watergate, civil rights—changed from tie-dyes to neckties as making money and owning a piece of the rock became driving forces in our society. Success became the ultimate goal, and in the eighties that meant a mad rush to gain power, prestige, and financial wealth. But despite this focus on individual success, the decade closed with a widespread sense of discontent, as if our collective spirit were crying out, "Is this all there is? If this is success, why don't I feel more fulfilled, more alive—more successful?"

We are starving for something more, something *beyond success* as we move toward the next millennium. We no longer want to simply make a living; we want to make a difference—to make contributions that extend well beyond ourselves. The "me generation" is searching for ways to transform into the "we generation." We desperately want our children to inherit a much better world than the one our parents left to us.

Yet, despite a growing hunger for hope, possibility, and belief in our potential we encounter a daily reality filled with apprehension, aggression, and doubt. We want to live truly winning lives—alight with love, friendship, adventure, and energy—but we wonder if we really can. Sadly, the secrets that can unlock the unique genius within each of us are often hidden even from ourselves behind walls of fear and limitation.

In this book you will find keys to help you break through the obstacles that stand between you and your dreams. My purpose is to guide and inspire you to greater fulfillment, inner satisfaction, and peace of mind than you've ever experienced—to help you move beyond success. Along the way I will challenge several deeply ingrained cultural belief systems that subtly and constantly bolster our fears while stifling our strengths. Three of these beliefs can be particularly damaging until we take charge and choose our own direction.

The first is our belief about success itself. Though lip service is sometimes given to the importance of participation, effort, and improvement in defining success, deep down most people still evaluate their success by what others think, not by what they feel within themselves. As long as we believe even slightly that success is determined externally, we open the door for a paralyzing fear of failure. We place ourselves at the effect rather than at the cause of our experience. In our society we have set things up so that very few people win while everyone else "loses." As long as this definition of success and failure remains dominant in our culture, blame, conflict, and irresponsibility will flourish. But when we change this foundational belief at a heart level, we will gain back the freedom to take responsibility for our own experience. We open a window of opportunity to live a winning life.

The second belief we will challenge concerns our basic ideas about leadership. Today's political, social, business, and educational leaders live under the constant glare of media spotlights. The combination of rampant negative campaigning; sensationalized storytelling in television, radio, and printed media; and acts of bona fide greed, dishonesty, and selfishness by some public and corporate officials has resulted in rapidly growing disrespect for leadership. We are teaching ourselves and our children that leaders are not to be trusted. This epidemic of declining faith has left most of us (the common, everyday people) wanting to have as little as possible to do with them (those scoundrels collectively known as leaders).

The tragedy in this "us-against-them" scenario is that a more fundamental and important truth has become nearly invisible, obscured by our rage, doubt, or, worse yet, indifference. This truth is simply that every one of us is a leader. In every moment we have the opportunity to decide what is next for us. Making decisions is the essence of leadership. We must dispel the disempowering belief that leadership is the unwanted burden of a dishonest, power-hungry elite, and replace it with an inspired and energetic acceptance that *the gift of personal leadership is our most basic birthright.* When we do this, we invigorate our lives with newfound exuberance and vitality. We regain respect and appreciation for the courage that is required to step forward and lead. We rediscover that we can truly make a difference.

The gift of personal leadership is our most basic birthright.

The third belief we will examine and refine concerns our foundational understanding of teams. Though most of us love the idea of being part of a team, we often use the team concept to separate rather than connect. Even within our own companies, families, and social organizations, we create subgroups that pit us against each other, fueling the fire of animosity while diminishing the resources that would otherwise be available to us if we expanded our view of teams rather than restricting it. When we deepen our level of consideration for others, we begin to honor differences instead of fearing them. As we become unconditional team players we realize that our toughest competitors are often our most empowering teammates. Their competition helps to bring out the very best in us.

The concepts, strategies, and philosophies that make up the fifteen secrets are as applicable in the classroom and the family room as they are in the boardroom. You will find these principles to be straightforward and grounded in common sense. Taken together, they create a rock-solid foundation on which to build a new pathway to inner satisfaction and peace of mind.

Within each chapter you will discover the possibility of profound, positive advancement in every facet of your life. As you put these ideas to work, I ask you to hold firm to your belief in the possibility of positive change. Possibility is the thread you use to weave your life's purpose and vision. Without positive reinforcement, it can sometimes wear very thin. But no matter how thin you stretch this thread of possibility, there is only one way it can break—by giving up hope.

Thank you for allowing me to explore with you new dimensions that will enhance the quality of your life. As we uncover each of the fifteen secrets of a winning life, we will create a plan to nurture and develop the immense potential you already possess. As I work with individuals and businesses from manufacturing to service industries, I am constantly struck by the power of these simple, commonsense philosophies to transform mayhem into motion, doubt into clear direction. They will provide you with a compass to navigate the uncharted waters of tomorrow with peace and confidence. Enjoy every precious moment.

1

Pygmalion:
Expectation and Reality

L ong ago on the Island of Cyprus there lived a great king, Pygmalion. He yearned for companionship and love, but, alas, he was very much alone.

One day he set out to create a sculpture of a beautiful woman. All of the loneliness and emotion that had built up inside him spilled out as he poured his heart and soul into his work. When he finished, he had created a graceful figure of such beauty and life that he fell deeply in love with it. More than anything on earth, he wanted his sculptured woman to come to life so that he could spend every waking moment with her. With his heart nearly bursting, he prayed to the Greek goddess of love, Aphrodite, to grant his wish.

Pygmalion was a very good man, so Aphrodite decided to help him. She descended to earth and magically transformed the cold stone into a living, breathing woman of incredible warmth and beauty. Her name was Galatea, and she and Pygmalion were married and lived happily ever after.

This wonderful legend from Greek mythology describes a foundational element of leadership and the essence of empowerment. The term *Pygmalion effect* describes the transformative power of expectation. *As we communicate the vision we have for others and the expectations we hold for them, we create an almost magnetic pull that draws them in the direction of those expectations.* We communicate these feelings and expectations, both positive and negative, through our words, our voice qualities, and our body language.

How Expectations Become Reality

The Pygmalion effect has been substantiated in a number of studies through the years. A researcher from Harvard University, Robert Rosenthal, presented dramatic evidence of the impact of the Pygmalion effect. He went to elementary classes and informed teachers that he was administering a test that would identify academic potential. In reality, the test was a sham. Rosenthal proceeded to identify to the teachers a number of students (actually chosen completely at random) as exceptionally talented young people who would excel if given strong direction and support. By the end of the school year, the overwhelming majority of children Rosenthal identified to the teachers as "spurters" had improved both their IQ scores and their grades dramatically. The reason was simple: the phony test scores raised the teachers' expectations of these students. As a result, the teachers taught the randomly selected children as if they were something special. Every aspect of the teachers' behavior communicated their belief in these children. Rosenthal went on to perform similar studies with welding students at the community college level, and the results were just as striking.

The Pygmalion effect is real. As we communicate our expectations of others, we influence their expectations of themselves. The more important our position in the eyes of others, the more powerful our influence. It is critical that we realize the importance of the Pygmalion effect, because it can either build or destroy.

As we communicate our expectations of others, we influence their expectations of themselves.

In the early 1970s, a Stanford psychology professor named David Rosenhan presented findings from a stunning experiment he had conducted over a period of two years. To discover the impact on patients of the social and physical environment in mental institutions, Rosenhan and several associates were admitted to various mental hospitals as diagnosed schizophrenics. No one but the chief medical officers and administrators of the hospitals knew the researchers' true identities.

On the day he was admitted, Rosenhan sat quietly in the schizophrenic ward of the hospital. He was still dressed in slacks and a sweater because he had not yet received the regular hospital gown worn by patients. An attendant who apparently mistook him for a visitor or a doctor initiated a conversation with Rosenhan. They had a stimulating and friendly discussion for quite some time until one of the nurses on the ward spotted the attendant and gestured for him to approach her. Rosenhan overheard her explaining to the attendant that he was a new patient and needed the appropriate hospital clothing.

Rosenhan spent many months in the hospital and saw the attendant virtually every day. *Yet from the moment the nurse identified Rosenhan as a patient, the attendant never again said a word to him!* During Rosenhan's stay he carried a notebook with him, jotting down endless, detailed notes of his observations. Not one staff member, doctor, nurse, or attendant ever asked what he was writing. A new expectation of him had been established the moment he had been admitted. He was no longer a human being; he was a schizophrenic. Every behavior directed his way was based on this expectation. Rosenhan's colleagues in other hospitals reported strikingly similar findings.

In Anticipation of Greatness:
Building Teams

Every great parent, coach, teacher, and leader is a powerful *positive* Pygmalion, keenly aware of the importance of never underestimating others. There is untapped greatness in all of us. As leaders, our foremost responsibility is to help our team members discover and develop their special qualities. This means we often must see others' brilliance before they see it themselves. We must hold the image of excellence up to them so they begin to see themselves in that light.

Coach John Wooden, the legendary UCLA basketball coach, is an extraordinary modern-day Pygmalion. He believed steadfastly in his people, treating them with dignity and respect. It was natural for him to help others feel important because he knew they truly were. He expected his players to be students first and foremost, and communicated that expectation constantly in both words and actions. As a result, the graduation rate for his players was well over 95 percent—far better than for the student population as a whole. Many of his players went on to achieve success in a variety of fields, from business to medicine to education.

Coach Wooden often described his team as a finely tuned automobile. The top scorer or "star" of the team is the engine. But, no matter how powerful your engine is, you won't get very far if you don't have any wheels. Great scorers need ball handlers and passers to get them the ball. Those who play tenacious defense and put the ball in the scorer's hands are the wheels. And what of the players at the end of the bench who rarely get in the game? They are the nuts and bolts that hold the wheels in place. Without someone to push the starters in practice and fully support them in the games, the starters could easily lose their sharpness and concentration. Thus, every member of the team is important, from the players on the court to the people who pick up the towels in the locker room. And no one knows when each team member will have the greatest impact: the greatest element in stardom is the rest of the team.

Like John Wooden, I began my professional career as an athletic coach. For eight years I had the joy of coaching competitive swimming in San Fernando Valley, California. I didn't work with a school team, but was a United States Swimming coach. This meant that I worked with athletes not just for a season or a semester, but year-round. I coached some kids for eight straight years; I became a real part of these young people's lives. It was an incredible experience.

No one knows when each team member will have the greatest impact: the greatest element in stardom is the rest of the team.

Over the course of those eight years we grew from a tiny novice team to one of the largest privately owned swimming teams in the country, numbering over two hundred swimmers. We earned national recognition by placing in the top ten at both the Senior and Junior National Championships. More than forty of our athletes earned college scholarships to schools across the country, from the University of Hawaii to the University of Miami. Some of our top performers participated in the Olympic Trials and international competitions.

An Unforgettable Lesson

This experience taught me much, and one of my most unforgettable lessons came through a swimmer named Allison. Allison was definitely not one of the "stars." Although a part of our team for many years, she never achieved any great honors. She was short and slight of build, yet very big of heart, and she had bright red hair like Little Orphan Annie. (It took a real effort to stuff that curly mass into her swimming cap each day!) I simply adored her. She always came to practice with an upbeat attitude and a determination to work as hard as she could. She was utterly unselfish and constantly supported and encouraged her teammates.

In local age-group swimming the major goal for the kids was to qualify for the Junior Olympics. Age-group swimming was like a roller coaster: just as the kids reached the top of their age group, their birthdays would come, they'd move to an older age group, and they'd find themselves at the bottom of the heap all over again. Allison had been close to qualifying for the Junior Olympics a couple of times, but had always just missed before she "aged up." She never gave up trying, though!

Finally, Allison made it! In my last summer as a coach, she qualified for the Junior Olympics in one event, the hundred-meter butterfly. She hit the time standard on the nose—one one-hundredth of a second slower and she would not have qualified. I was sure this was the pinnacle of her swimming career. All of us were thrilled that she had made it and would finally have the chance to participate in this prestigious competition. I was especially

13

pleased because this was to be my very last meet as a coach. I had announced to the team that I was leaving swimming to attend graduate school at UCLA, so it was a very emotional time for the kids and me.

Allison was a perfect example of what coaches call a "drop-dead sprinter." She had good natural speed but would inevitably "tie up" toward the end of her races. Over and over again I would watch her burst to a great start, then struggle painfully as kids passed her in the final few strokes. It was as if a baby grand piano had fallen on her back. Exhausted, she would struggle out of the pool and walk dejectedly over to see me.

It has been said that the definition of insanity is doing the same thing over and over and expecting a different result. If you looked up insanity in the dictionary, you probably would have seen my picture during those years because every time Allison came to me for support and encouragement after a painful race, I said the same ridiculous thing. "Allison," I'd say in my most inspirational coaching voice, "one of these days you're not going to die!" Great coaching, huh? Then I'd give her a big hug just to lock in those feelings and send her off to loosen up. Off she'd go, her body in knots and her mind filled with thoughts of "dying." If I give you the instruction, "Don't think of the number three," what happens? Automatically, three pops into your mind. The more you try to push it away, the more you see it. Unwittingly, I was consistently directing both Allison and myself toward a belief she would die at the end of her races. I was a well-meaning, yet highly effective *negative* Pygmalion!

Many people have the mistaken impression that swimming is an individual sport. After all, once you dive into that water you're seemingly alone. Nothing, however, could be further from the truth. My many years as a coach taught me that swimming is an extraordinary team sport. Every day, these kids trained together, pouring their hearts out, challenging, encouraging, and supporting one another. The sense of unity this created—which I shall discuss later as the "relay paradigm"—connected them in spirit and energy level. At some workouts and competitions, it was as if the pool flowed downhill. Each athlete gathered strength from the others and everyone flew! On other days, however, everyone seemed to catch an identical case of "slow-motion sickness."

"Allison," I'd say in my most inspirational coaching voice, "one of these days you're not going to die!"

Our team focused on Junior Olympics as our top team competition. In the strongest age-group swimming region in the world, we perennially finished second to mighty Mission Viejo in California. We had a huge contingent of swimmers who had qualified for the older age-group Junior Olympics and, on paper, we looked like a

15

strong second place finisher once again. Since this meet was my last, the kids wanted to send me out with a special performance. Emotions ran high as the meet approached.

Allison's event turned out to be the first of the meet. What's more, as the slowest qualifier, she would compete in the first heat of the event. With sixty-four girls in the 100-meter butterfly, that meant she would be in heat one, lane eight, right next to the edge of the pool.

We always warmed up the same way at competitions. First I sent the kids off on a long, easy loosen-up swim to stretch their muscles and get the feel of the pool. After they had sufficiently warmed up, I timed the kids in short sprints. They were fresh and psyched up, so they usually turned in some excellent times.

As Allison approached the starting block for her sprint, she shined like a beam of light. She was so excited about finally being at Junior Olympics that she was supercharged. As the slowest qualifier in her race she felt no real pressure—just pure, unabashed joy at being there. I signaled her to step up on the block and called out, "Ready, ho!" She exploded toward me with more speed and power than I had ever seen from her before. I clicked my stopwatch as she plowed by me at the 25-meter mark, and watched her face light up with a huge grin when I read her sprint time to her. It was by far the best she had ever done, and she absolutely bubbled with enthusiasm.

I don't know if it was the shock of her terrific sprint time or the look of excitement in her eyes, but something shook loose in my brain and a new idea burst forth. Remember, for seven years I had said the exact same thing to Allison over and over: "One of these days you're not going to die." But this time she looked so phenomenal in that sprint that I bent down close to her and put my hands on her shoulders. "Allison, that was fantastic! Do you remember how you just felt? Great! Remember how high you were on the water and how light and powerful you were?"

She could hardly keep her feet on the ground as she looked up at me and nodded excitedly. "Yeah, Coach. I felt awesome! I can't wait for my race!"

I don't know if it was the shock of her terrific sprint time or the look of excitement in her eyes, but something shook loose in my brain and a new idea burst forth.

I looked straight into her bright eyes. "Allison, when you dive into the water for your 100-meter butterfly, I want you to remember just how you felt in that sprint. I'll be standing right here, at the 75-meter mark. When you get to me with 25 meters to go, I'll yell, 'Now!' As soon as you hear me I want you to pretend that you just dove in to do that exact same sprint all over again. Can you see it?"

"Yes, Coach!"

"Can you feel it?"

"I got it, Coach!"

"Great!"

Sometimes the difference between mediocrity and unleashing the greatness inside you is very slight. As a leader, you may be right on the edge of becoming the catalyst to bring out the very best in your people. The possibility is there in every moment. Often the single most powerful action you can take is to help people focus on what they want—not what they don't want. When they become crystal clear and extremely specific about what they are shooting for, look out!

I sent Allison off to check in for her event and gathered the rest of the team together. Typically we'd send a big contingent down to the end of the pool to cheer for their teammates as they approached the turn. The sight of these crazy kids, yelling and screaming their lungs out, was often enough to ignite an extra burst of adrenaline. This time I decided to do something special, though. I instructed half the kids to head down to the end of the pool to cheer Allison on. But then I gathered the other half of the kids around me and showed them the 75-meter signal I had set up with Allison. I told them that when I gave the signal, I wanted them to let out the loudest NOW in history! I wanted that place to shake. We'd be right next to Allison so she would definitely get a jolt. If nothing else, we'd *scare* her into finishing stronger!

As she stepped up onto the blocks I could feel the hope and excitement of all her teammates. In a very real sense, they were right up there on the blocks with her. These kids had trained the same way as Allison and had prepared for this meet under the exact same system. If she did well, their confidence would soar. If she didn't, the kids would search for rational reasons, but for many, a little bit of their emotional edge would be lost.

Often the single most powerful action you can take is to help people focus on what they want—not what they don't want.

Allison had never felt so completely supported before. As she looked down to the end of the 50-meter pool, she saw at least fifty of her teammates enthusiastically clapping and cheering for her. Little red-haired Allison was ready to go!

When the gun fired, she took off like a shot. She looked terrific! By 25 meters she had opened up almost a full body-length's lead on the rest of the heat. As she closed in on the turn, every stroke seemed to pump up her teammates more. They went crazy, waving her on and cheering their lungs out. She exploded out of the turn and headed home with 50 meters to go. I checked my watch for her 50-meter time and thought, This is great! She can die and still do her best time!

As she approached the 75-meter mark, she continued to move strongly. She had well over two body-lengths on the nearest competitor. Then, something magical happened. Spontaneously, without any coaching from me, the fifty or so kids who had been cheering for her at the turn became so inspired by Allison's performance that they sprinted around the edge of the pool and joined the other kids gathered around me at 75 meters. We had almost one hundred wildly excited kids squeezed together waiting for my signal: 80 meters . . . 77 . . .

As she moved her head forward to breathe at 75 meters, I whipped my arm down. Together, one hundred voices joined in a window-rattling "NOW!"

I will always remember what happened next. This little girl, who had died in race after race, and who I simply adored, suddenly climbed up on top of the water like a hydroplane! She exploded toward the finish with more speed and strength than I thought possible. With eight strokes to go she took her last breath. Head down and every muscle driving, she blasted to the finish. As she touched the wall, she looked over to her right but didn't see any other swimmers. She told me later that she thought they had already finished and climbed out!

I looked at my watch and froze. She had dropped her time more than 10 seconds! For years I had watched her struggle out of the water, totally exhausted as she finished her races. Now, though, as she heard her time, she leaped out of the water like an Olympic gymnast. She bounded over to me with a huge grin and more than enough energy to swim the race all over again! Her teammates buzzed with excitement. It was my peak moment as a coach.

Something almost magical happens when people break through the obstacles that hold them back and discover what is truly inside them. *At this moment, they move from hoping to knowing.* It is the most electrifying and empowering of all transformations. The impact on their teammates is no less dramatic. The experience of seeing one of their own achieve what they are truly capable of awakens a heightened belief in their own potential.

Something almost magical

happens when people break

through the obstacles that

hold them back and discover

what is truly inside them.

As Allison bounced over to the warm-down pool, her father walked shakily toward me with a stunned look on his face. I had known him for years. He was a very calm, soft-spoken man. I knew how much he loved

Allison because he attended every event, quietly supporting her. But I had never seen him express much emotion, either verbally or physically.

When he reached me, he put his arms around me and hugged me tightly. Tears streamed down his cheeks. I felt my eyes mist over as he looked at me with astonishment and gratitude. "What did you do to her?" he asked.

I responded with something brilliant like, "I have no idea." Then I said something that did make sense: *"She did it."* He squeezed me again and wandered off.

Allison's remarkable swim had taken place in the first of eight qualifying heats. The top sixteen girls would return that night for the consolations and the finals. When the last of the eight heats finished, Allison had moved from sixty-fourth to first!

That evening, Allison came back and swam a whale of a race. She improved her time another two-tenths of a second over her unbelievable morning performance. She was touched out on the very last stroke and finished second. But there has never been a truer winner.

As the meet progressed, our kids seemed to be ignited by what I have since come to call the "Allison factor." Race after race, Allison's teammates sped to tremendous improvements over their personal bests. When the final team points were totaled, we had pulled an upset and won the older age-group Junior Olympics.

Later, when I had a chance to sort out this remarkable event, I realized that some amazing truths had been revealed. Until then, I had prided myself on knowing exactly what my swimmers were capable of. If I had been asked to pick the one swimmer on my team least likely to be our leader at the Junior Olympics, it would have been Allison. After all, she had only one event and was seeded dead last. I had been sure that just qualifying for the meet would be the pinnacle of her swimming career and that with luck, she might be able to improve her time a few tenths of a second. But there was no way on earth I would have believed she could drop ten seconds in a 100-meter race.

Race after race, Allison's teammates sped to tremendous improvements over their personal bests.

Allison taught me to never underestimate what we have inside. The people we think we know the best are the ones who can most surprise us when they surpass the limitations they—*and we*—have set for them. *There are no overachievers; we all have an almost infinite supply of potential.* Believing this creates great openness, flexibility, and sensitivity in the way you look at the people you work with and serve. As with Pygmalion, what you look for in others and yourself, you will find. And what you find, you will unleash.

2

Vision:
Knowing What's Important

Perhaps no leader in modern times has earned and received more consistent respect and admiration from virtually everyone connected with his field than John Wooden. His players—whether superstars like Kareem Abdul-Jabbar and Bill Walton, or backups who rarely made it into a game—revered him with equal intensity. He is cited as an example of excellence in countless business books on subjects from Total Quality Management to leadership. Even the news media treated him with an unusually high degree of respect, though he is quick to point out with a twinkle in his eye that before his first NCAA Championship in 1964, he was known as the coach who couldn't beat Cal! Today, many years since his retirement from coaching, past players, assistant coaches, alumni supporters, and university officials still frequently call him seeking his counsel and guidance.

Through it all, from humble beginnings as an Indiana farm boy to the height of his career as the unquestioned champion of his field, John Wooden maintained a remarkably balanced perspective. He always managed to keep the long term in view, building within each individual who worked with him an unparalleled level of trust in his leadership.

Face to Face and Heart to Heart

When I first decided to contact Coach Wooden in 1991 to arrange an interview, I had very clear objectives in mind. First and foremost, I was determined to be a sponge: to absorb a deep understanding of the foundational philosophies, beliefs, and strategies by which he lives so that I could share them with others. I was also excited about learning these fundamentals for myself.

I had always considered myself a team builder. In every position in which I had served through the years, from athletics as a United States Swimming coach to business as an executive in the transportation industry and later in the training and development field, I firmly believed that my success was directly derived from my ability to bring out the best in those around me. When I had the opportunity to foster greater teamwork in organizations throughout the world through my writing, speaking, and seminars, I felt a strong sense of responsibility to learn from the very best. To me, this was the opportunity of a lifetime: the chance to sit down and talk with the greatest coach in history, face to face and heart to heart.

Coach Wooden greeted me warmly, and we walked together into his apartment. He lives quite modestly, as material wealth has never been a high priority in his life. (He often says, "True happiness comes from the things that can't be taken away.") As we sat down I scanned his home, fascinated to drink in every detail of our time together. In an instant, many clues to the priorities that motivate Coach Wooden were evident. Everywhere I saw pictures and mementos of family—of his lovely wife, Nellie, and of their children, grandchildren, and great-grandchildren. Very few of the hundreds of awards he had won over the years were displayed. Indeed, the "trophies" that have real meaning for him are his family treasures and his books. He is a ravenous reader with hundreds of novels, books of poetry, biographies, and spiritual volumes filling his shelves. For just a moment before we began, I allowed myself to revel in this experience. Here I was, in John Wooden's living room, about to learn all I could from the coach who set the standard of leadership for all others.

This was the opportunity of a lifetime: the chance to sit down and talk with the greatest coach in history, face to face and heart to heart.

As we began, Coach Wooden guided me back to his roots. He grew up on a small southern Indiana farm. On the day he graduated from the one-room country school where he received his basic education, his father gave him a piece of paper with a simple creed written on it. Wooden has carried that creed with him ever since.

John Wooden's Seven-Point Creed

1. **Be true to yourself.**

2. **Make friendship a fine art.**

3. **Make each day your masterpiece.**

4. **Build a shelter against a rainy day.**

5. **Help others.**

6. **Drink deeply from good books.**

7. **Pray for guidance and give thanks for your blessings every day.**

This creed had an immense impact on Wooden, who was a terribly shy and quiet young man. These simple yet powerful words awakened in him a vision of leadership, and the remarkable consistency that would mark his illustrious career stemmed from the clear direction this seven-point vision gave him. Throughout his life, it served him equally well during the best and the most difficult of times. The seven points became like a strong rope across the rushing river of life. As he inched his way across, regardless of the power of the torrent below, he knew success would come if he kept firm to the rope. Each time he reached forward and grasped the rope, his balance became stronger and his fear of the river less paralyzing. Even when the river threatened to swallow him up with icy cold water, he focused on the rope, tightened his grip, and renewed his strength. Such is the mobilizing power of a compelling vision.

Coach Wooden has spent a lifetime working to deepen the internalization of this vision. He has sought to live all of the seven points each and every day—personally, professionally, and spiritually. Through time, the creed has evolved into more than a vision: it has become his identity. As the personification of the "principle-centered leader" that Stephen Covey writes so brilliantly about in his book, *Principle-Centered Leadership*, Coach Wooden communicates his vision to every individual with whom he comes in contact in the most powerful way possible—through the unstoppable force of his being.

Define, Live, and Communicate Your Vision

Vision is the essential, ever-present element in the regenerating life cycle that allows us to go beyond success. The cycle begins by *defining* a personal vision. This is the seed of great leadership. *Living* that vision to the very best of your ability each day—gradually transforming vision to identity—is the process of growth for great leadership. *Communicating* that vision and identity consistently and naturally to others so they may begin to cultivate their own vision is the bud of new leadership. At this point, a single vision has become the flower that reseeds an ever-growing garden.

When you consider that 53 percent of the companies from the 1980 Fortune 500 no longer exist, the consequences of short-term or nonexistent vision become shockingly clear. Yet as I work with both large and small companies it becomes increasingly apparent that rarely is a solid, centering vision present, and even more rarely is it communicated in ways that inspire others to ignite their own compelling visions. In our world of explosively accelerating technology and dizzying rates of change, it is critical that we reassess the very fundamentals of how we conduct ourselves as we guide our organizations.

Today's leadership must learn to be far more concerned with *empowerment* than with *power*. The essence of empowerment is the three-stage vision process so clearly demonstrated by Coach Wooden's example.

1. Define the vision.
2. Live the vision (transform vision into identity).
3. Communicate the vision consistently to catalyze new leadership.

Championship results are an inevitable product of this fundamental leadership formula.

The importance of vision became vividly clear to me when I worked with a large telecommunications company. My training company was consulted because this organization—comprised of thousands of talented, bright, capable people—had experienced an attitudinal shift that was both disempowering and debilitating. The rampant uncertainty surrounding layoffs and restructuring had severely challenged the free spirit, boldness, fun, and unshakable confidence that had been a foundation of the organization. The group we were asked to work with was gathered together because they, more than anybody else in the organization, had fought to keep spirit and inspired vision alive. Yet even among these caring managers, trepidation, political uncertainty, and heartfelt pain at the loss or potential loss of teammates had begun to negatively affect results. Momentum had slowed because focus had shifted from vision to contingency plans and survival strategies.

Today's leadership must learn to be far more concerned with *empowerment* than with *power*.

When we interviewed these managers, an important question surfaced. Do vision and attitude drive results, or do results drive vision and attitude? In other words, which comes first, the winner's mind-set or the win?

It is clear that the mind-set and results work together either to build contagious positive momentum or to sap virtually all organizational vitality and initiative. The more we listened to these talented and intelligent managers, the clearer it became that they had been waiting for the wins to revitalize their vision. They were paralyzed, staring down at the rapids below. And their grip was beginning to slip from the rope. The entire game plan we created for them was based on the conviction that the mind-set, ignited by vision and carried forward through attitudes and beliefs, generates the wins. This is the combination of factors each of us must focus on in building success, because these are the elements we can most control.

Over the course of a two-day workshop, we began to guide the managers through the three-stage vision process. Each individual emerged from a series of activities with the first draft of his or her own personal vision statement. The impact of even that first step—defining a personal vision—was immediate and profound. It was as if the participants had finally found their car keys after one of those agonizing searches we've all experienced when we're in a great hurry and can't find them anywhere. As the managers completed their first draft of their personal vision statements, they took their places back at the wheel. Their engines were running and they were on the road again. They would undoubtedly encounter traffic jams, detours, and even a few fender benders as they began stage two, the process of *living* their vision. But, compared to the paralysis and frustration they had felt when they couldn't even find the keys, these obstacles were far less intimidating.

Creating Success Beyond Compare

Coach Wooden is best remembered for the final twelve years of his coaching career, 1963 to 1975, the period when his personal vision process reached full bloom.

During those twelve years all of his ten NCAA Championships were won. Yet Coach Wooden would be the first to tell you that without the first two stages— defining a personal vision, then living it—the third stage, communicating it, would not have been possible. It was during the long process of stage two, as he conscientiously sought to live his seven-point creed, that he gradually transformed his vision into his identity. It was then that the specifics in his philosophy of leadership came into focus. Coach Wooden's seven-point creed provided him with a vision of a way to live and to lead.

As he worked at bringing the vision to life within himself, he found he hungered for greater clarity about *where* the vision led. He wanted success and believed deeply that living his seven-point creed would move him irrepressibly toward achieving it. But what was this goal called success? It is a term often used, but rarely defined. How could he achieve success if he didn't know specifically what it meant to him? He had determined a direction for his life, but had yet to identify the destination.

But what was this goal called success? It is a term often used, but rarely defined.

Throughout his childhood, his father had impressed on him a very simple, fundamental rule that eventually led to his definition of success. His is a definition that differs radically from most I have encountered because this underlying rule—*Never compare yourself to others*—goes against one of the most pervasive, conditioned habits in our culture: comparison for the purpose of self-evaluation. When we compare ourselves to others, we direct our focus toward that which we cannot control. If we feel successful only when we outscore, outsell, or outperform others, we tend to set ourselves up for either failure or self-aggrandizement. Neither serves us well over time.

Upon his graduation from Purdue University in 1934, Coach Wooden expanded his rule of never comparing into a definition of success that became the destination he has focused on throughout his life. As a parent, a coach, and a leader, this definition crystallized the vision of success he worked to instill first within himself, and then within all those he touched.

3

Character:
Redefining Success

"Success is peace of mind that is a direct result of self-satisfaction in knowing you gave your best effort to become the best of which you are capable."

—JOHN WOODEN

I t is essential that we consider Coach Wooden's definition of success very carefully before we begin to explore each of the fifteen secrets. There is much more here than initially meets the eye. This is the centerpiece of everything John Wooden strived for as a coach, leader, and human being and is the critical component in expanding hope for our future as a global family. His ultimate goal—peace of mind—is not something that can be measured on a scoreboard or immortalized in a Hall of Fame. Neither is it something that can be attained only by a select few at the end of a project, a season, or even a career. Instead, it goes beyond success because it is possible for each one of us in any moment. Though others may sense its presence in us, *only we can truly know it for ourselves in our own hearts*. It is not about actually *achieving* the best of which we are capable; that would lead to an endlessly unfulfilling pursuit of perfection.

Instead, it is about truly enjoying the process of growing and feeling deeply satisfied that we have given our best.

Success is not something that can be attained only by a select few at the end of a project, a season, or even a career.

You may find it surprising to learn that in twenty-seven years as the coach of UCLA basketball, John Wooden never used the word *winning!* He believed winning was not in his or his players' control. Instead, he constantly instilled his definition of success within himself and his teams. By living according to this view, the opportunity to go beyond success was possible in every moment, regardless of outside circumstances. This was a new paradigm in the athletic world, and one he had to reinforce constantly. The press, alumni, and most of his peers defined success by the scoreboard, but under Coach Wooden's tutelage players were taught that the control and the responsibility for success lay within themselves. They learned to focus on becoming *their* best. In Wooden's system, winning championships and earning recognition as "the best" were valued by-products, but not the focal point.

Measuring Up

As a young English teacher and athletic coach at a South Bend, Indiana high school, Wooden became concerned about the way parents tended to judge their children and him as their teacher. As he put it:

> The good Lord in his infinite wisdom did not create us all equal when it comes to size, strength, appearance, or various aptitudes. Some children put out a great effort to earn a C in my English class. In my mind, these children deserved to feel successful. They were putting forth the effort to be the best of which they were capable. But parents didn't see it that way. No, a C grade was not all right for their child. Either something must be wrong with that teacher, or their child must be sloughing off.

Most troubling to Wooden was the effect this had on the students. They began to feel second-rate. As their confidence faded, so did their performance.

He saw the same pattern in athletics. Only so many youngsters make the starting team. Yet, to many parents, something was dreadfully wrong if their child was not named a starter. It didn't seem to matter that the child was giving his or her all each day in practice and was really contributing to the team. If the child was not chosen to start, either the child, the coach, or both were considered failures.

The real damage came from the accumulation of these judgments over time. All too often, Wooden saw his students look at themselves as losers, not as having lost a game. Perhaps they had been outscored by an opponent with superior ability. It didn't seem to matter that they had played their hearts out or had improved markedly. To these young people and their parents, the scoreboard (or, for that matter, the report card) determined success or failure.

Following years of seeing students demoralized and their talents whittled away by this destructive pattern of criticism and comparison, Coach Wooden created the definition of success he still holds today.

I experienced firsthand the powerful positive ramifications of this alternative success paradigm during my years in the air freight industry. I was recruited by Lynden Air Freight at an extremely difficult time for the company, when the majority of its business was oil-related. The company had built a strong position in a specialized niche, providing air freight service from the domestic forty-eight states to Alaska. Just before I joined the company, the OPEC cartel in the Middle East made decisions that sent the price of oil plummeting. Overnight, the price had fallen more than $20 to less than $10 a barrel. Oil-related construction immediately slowed to a near standstill. So did the bulk of our air freight business.

I was brought onboard to assist with strategic planning and productivity enhancement just before every employee in the company took a cut in pay. In the two months prior to my being hired, several individuals had lost their jobs because of the sharp downturn in business.

As I listened to the people in the organization it

became apparent that their central focus had shifted to the outside, away from factors they could directly affect. Virtually every business conversation centered on the depressed marketplace, decreasing cargo space to Alaska, and the bottom-line question of whether there would be any jobs tomorrow.

The president of the company was a person of energy and vision. He was willing to take some risks to ignite positive change. At a time when most leaders would disdain so-called extra expenses for personal development training, new marketing campaigns, enhanced systems for measurement and communication, and incentive compensation opportunities for all employees, he was ready to take action. He allowed my team to implement an ongoing communication program focused on shifting the mind-set of our entire organization away from what was happening to us from the outside to what we could make happen on the inside.

The results were astonishing. Every aspect of the organization improved dramatically and rapidly. Over the next three years the company nearly quadrupled its sales while diversifying its customer base by opening several new market niches. For the first time in its history, Lynden received national recognition as a leader in customer service and convenience. On-time delivery performance soared, and consistent profitability was achieved. Even more important, internal recognition and acknowledgment became a constant in the organization as teammates expressed their genuine appreciation for one another.

For the first time in its history, Lynden received national recognition as a leader in customer service and convenience.

Through that simple shift in focus, every member of the organization felt more consistently successful. People viewed themselves as valuable contributors to a quality team.

Coach Wooden's definition of success has just as profound an impact on the personal level as in the business context. As I was growing up, I learned the hard way about the pain and fear that come from an external focus on success.

What—or Who—Determines Your Success or Failure?

Like most young boys, I idolized my father. He was my hero. He was a tall, strong policeman with an intensity about him that commanded respect. More than anything on earth, I wanted to hear my dad tell me how much he loved me. I wanted him to hug me and longed to know deep down inside that he thought I was a great kid. Without realizing it, I had created a definition of success for myself that depended on recognition from my father.

The trouble was, Dad was a man who kept most of his emotions tightly holed-up inside him. He had lost his mother at a very young age, and much of the gentle, loving side of him seemed to have gone with her. He was tough, solemn, and disciplined. He worked incredibly hard, and to bring in extra money, he often took on construction jobs in addition to his forty-plus hours a week as a police officer. Only when I grew much older did I realize that this was the only way he could express his love and devotion to us. He simply could not tell us in words or through any display of physical affection how he felt.

As more and more desperately I yearned to receive my dad's love and respect, a deep and driving desire to prove myself took hold of me. I absolutely had to be the best in everything I did. In school, athletics, even in gaining popularity, I never felt complete unless I was number one.

On the surface, the results of this intense drive seemed outstanding. I did well enough to be accepted to Stanford University and to excel there. Yet I found myself becoming terribly afraid to try new things. When I did well, the feeling of success was fleeting. Instead of enjoying self-satisfaction and peace of mind, I was terrified that I might not measure up again. I was far more concerned about what others thought of me than about who I really was.

After years of trying futilely to prove I was worthy of my father's love and respect, I finally reached a breaking point. Virtually every aspect of my life came to a screeching halt as I struggled to decide what I would do upon graduation from Stanford. I had neither interviewed for any jobs nor applied to graduate school. Subconsciously, I was paralyzed by an intense fear of failure.

At the same time, my two best friends had both begun close relationships with women. Instead of feeling elated for them, I found myself despondent, sinking into a quicksand of jealousy, self-pity, and loneliness. I could not bring myself to believe that my friends could love others without somehow losing their love for me.

After weeks of pain and struggle I hit bottom. My studies began to suffer as I lost the inspiration to hit the books. I became moody and sarcastic. Finally, I blew up at my friends over nothing. I was imploding from a deep sense of worthlessness. I felt so ashamed of my outburst that I jumped in my van and drove away. I felt I could never show my face again. When your self-worth comes from others instead of from inside, there is no more painful experience than humiliation. When that humiliation is self-imposed, the pain is even more intense.

I drove deep into the woods, blinking back tears that wouldn't seem to stop. Finally, I pulled over beside a little stream next to a deserted dirt road. There wasn't another soul around. I sat very still, listening to the trickle of the water. The quiet seemed to calm me, and I decided to write down my thoughts. I began slowly at first, then years of pent-up fear and doubt flowed out in a gush of emotion.

As I wrote, I found myself searching for some key to understanding what was happening inside me. At first I was very hard on myself, berating my selfishness, insecurity, and jealousy. Before long, though, I stopped beating myself up and began to dig for the roots of my feelings instead. I saw how much I had been comparing myself with others to determine my value as a person. For the first time, I became consciously aware of how deeply I longed to receive my father's love. I began to understand that much of my drive to achieve stemmed from that intense hunger for recognition and approval.

In the wake of this flood of honest emotion, I realized for the first time that throughout my whole life I had strived to be loved by others without truly feeling worthy of loving myself. A new clarity came to me about learning to accept myself. I wrote,

No one can be loved until they let themselves be seen.
No one can be seen until they learn to love themselves.

A deep and lasting change took place within me as the words poured out. It was a simple change on the surface, but one that would completely alter the direction of my life. I consciously decided to switch from striving to be the best, and to work instead toward becoming *my best*. It was as if the weight of the world was lifted from my shoulders. For the first time in my life, I stopped worrying about being the greatest and focused instead on being *me*.

The Difference Between Character and Reputation

Without knowing it at the time, I had taken a major step in the direction of true leadership. Coach Wooden's definition of success leads to concentration on character, not reputation. One of his favorite teachings is, "Be more concerned with your character than your reputation because your character is what you really are, while your reputation is merely what others think you are."

In order to go beyond success, you must focus on character that builds leadership. It is a natural and automatic focus when you derive your feelings of success from the inner knowledge that you've given the effort to be the best of which you're capable. Without it, you will be motivated by what you hope to receive rather than what you want to give. You will be far more concerned with credit than with teamwork.

Your team evaluates your honesty and trustworthiness based not on what you say as much as what you do. As a leader, you cannot hide your true motivations. Eventually, reputation-based leadership will be seen as self-serving and insincere. Conversely, people respond to character-based leadership with trust and loyalty. In study after study, honesty has been identified as the quality people within organizations want most from their leaders. It is essential to building an atmosphere of trust. In their excellent book, *The Leadership Challenge: How to Get Extraordinary Things Done in Organizations,* James Kouzes and Barry Posner state:

> In every survey we conducted, honesty was selected more often than any other leadership characteristic. When you think about it, honesty is absolutely essential to leadership. After all, if we are to willingly follow someone, whether it be into battle or into the boardroom, we first want to assure ourselves that the person is worthy of our trust.

Character-based leaders behave with consistency, courage, and trust. Because they know that the scoreboard does not determine their value and effectiveness as leaders, they are eager to make the tough decision and to place a higher level of trust in their team. They are willing to risk looking for the best in others because they are not threatened by others' excellence.

4

A Structure for Internal Leadership

In *Chicken Soup for the Soul,* a collection of classic stories that touch the heart and elevate the spirit, Jack Canfield and Mark Victor Hansen tell of a Buddhist monastery in Thailand. For centuries this temple had housed a clay statue of a huge, smiling Buddha. The massive sculpture stood more than ten feet high with a circumference of better than six feet around its expansive belly.

In the mid-1950s the monks who lived at the monastery were told that they must relocate the statue because a new highway was to be built right through their temple. They arranged for a crane to carefully lift their sacred Buddha so they could move it to a new home. As they began to raise the giant idol, they were startled by its unexpected weight. When they felt it begin to crack they quickly set it down, hoping to avoid any further damage. To make matters worse, rain began to fall on the statue. The monks hurriedly covered it with a canvas tarp while they waited for the weather to clear.

When night fell, the head monk came out to check on the statue. As he shined his flashlight on the crack, something sparkly caught his eye. His curiosity aroused, he rushed back into the monastery to find a hammer and chisel. Carefully, he chipped away a small section around the crack. When he had opened a small hole he stood back in amazement.

He assembled a crew of his fellow monks, and, armed with hammers and chisels, they worked feverishly all through the night. When they had finished chipping away every last inch of clay, there stood before them a magnificent, solid-gold Buddha!

Later, historians pieced together the story of the Golden Buddha. Several centuries earlier, the temple in which the statue had rested was in grave danger of attack by an invading Burmese army. Fearing that their sacred monument would be looted, the monks had covered it with eight to twelve inches of clay, hoping the soldiers would see little value in an earthen idol. The army did indeed come, and killed every one of the monks. Thus, their secret remained concealed until that momentous day in 1957.

There stood before them a magnificent, solid-gold Buddha!

The Golden Buddha is a magnificent metaphor for the sometimes hidden genius in all of us. When you look at a tiny baby, its spirit shines straight through to your heart. There is no pretense, no fear, no withholding. But as we grow, we begin to cover this perfect internal foundation with all sorts of superfluous junk. From the time we are one or two years old, we hear more than twenty noes for every yes that comes our way. It is little wonder that as children grow, their pure "golden essence" can be plastered over, like the clay covering the ancient Buddha. Fear and doubt are the main ingredients in the mortar that can envelop us and stifle our confidence and trust. Over time the mortar can become so thick that our innate qualities fade from memory until they are completely hidden, like the Golden Buddha beneath the clay.

Had the head monk not looked very carefully in just the right place, the secret of the Golden Buddha would still remain hidden. Just as he followed the crack in the great statue as a guide to know where to begin using his hammer and chisel, we need a blueprint and the right tools to break through our layers of apprehension and self-doubt and free our own inner glow.

Idea + Detail + Action = Actualization

Here's an opportunity to have some fun testing your powers of observation. Look around you. Notice every object in your surroundings, every piece of furniture, everything on the walls, the floor, and the ceiling. Once you've completed this little inventory, ask yourself a question: What does every object and structure you observed have in common, aside from being located in the same general area?

All of the objects and structures you noticed were created in the same special place and forged from the same remarkable raw material. The special place is the

49

human mind, and the raw material is an *idea.* How does a formless, intangible idea materialize? What differentiates a thought that fades into a hidden memory from one that actually translates into physical reality? There are two key tools we must use to bring our ideas to life.

The combination of belief plus action creates experiences that ultimately lead to wisdom.

The first is *detail.* By adding greater and greater detail to an idea, we ignite the possibility of transformation. Think of any of the human-made items you noticed during your inventory a moment ago. Initially someone had an idea, say, for a place to sit. At this point it was simply a thought. But then, as the individual introduced greater specificity, the idea of a place to sit began to develop. Perhaps it was sketched, and color, dimension, shape, and style were added.

When the tools and materials were gathered to actually build the chair, the second tool of transformation was applied: *action.* When we develop an idea by visualizing with fine detail, we transform the thought into a belief. We then have a strong sense of knowing the idea is possible. But knowing without taking action falls short of realization. When we continually fail to act on our beliefs, we fall into the abyss of procrastination. Only through doing does an idea become a reality. It has been said that doing what we know, rather than knowing what to do, is what makes the difference. The combination of belief plus action creates experiences that ultimately lead to wisdom.

Just as your chair was built from this simple formula (Idea + Detail + Action = Actualization), so too can the natural leader within you be reawakened using this formula. Without adding a level of detail to crystallize your idea of leadership, it would remain an inert idea: you'd want to be a good leader, but would be unclear about the specific elements that constitute quality leadership. As you add the specifics, you will transform your abstract idea of leadership into a personal vision. As you take action, you will gain invaluable experiences of leadership. These experiences will enable you to refine your knowledge and to develop wisdom gradually. Your detailed vision provides a blueprint with which you can solidly evaluate your growth as a leader.

Using the Pyramid of Success to Build Dynamic Leadership

When Coach Wooden redefined success, he provided an ultimate goal for himself and all those who worked with him. This was not enough, however. He needed more detail to gauge the progress of his actions. Consequently, he spent fourteen years designing a very specific structure leading to this ultimate goal. The structure he envisioned was a pyramid, composed of fifteen essential building blocks. He believed deeply that by taking consistent action to develop his performance in each of these fifteen areas, he would constantly improve his ability to lead first himself and then others.

The Pyramid of Success

The Pyramid of Success provides a beginning blueprint to guide you toward the dynamic qualities within yourself and your team. With each block of the pyramid you will discover one of the fifteen secrets of a winning life. By creating a context for constructive self-evaluation, the pyramid simplifies the often confusing and sometimes overwhelming challenge of consistently improving the quality of your life. You will be able to use the pyramid to accelerate your advancement as a leader by identifying specific areas to strengthen. Ultimately, though, only by taking action and consistently working on fundamentals will you actually achieve your goals.

Focus on Fundamentals

Virtually every great teacher and coach throughout history has stressed the importance of fundamentals in all aspects of personal and professional life. Mahatma Gandhi established several fundamental disciplines that he practiced religiously as a way to strengthen his connection to his beliefs. Each day he walked four to six miles as the sun rose, wove at least two hundred yards of yarn into cloth, and maintained a very simple, healthful diet that kept him remarkably fit physically and mentally throughout his long life. Great coaches like Paul "Bear" Bryant, Vince Lombardi, Lou Holtz, and John Wooden eschewed fancy, flashy play in practices or games. Instead, they favored consistent focus on developing outstanding fundamental habits. As Anthony Robbins, the personal development teacher, often states, "Repetition is the mother of skill."

When using the pyramid as your road map to the fifteen secrets, three key fundamentals are most important.

1. Develop Inner Perspective

Personalize the pyramid by deciding which areas are most important for you to develop. Only you can evaluate your true progress in each block of the structure. The pyramid is something you use to develop character, not reputation.

2. Be an Example

If you are to lead others according to the system the pyramid defines and the secrets it unveils, it is critical that you lead *yourself* by those same principles. The familiar phrase, "Do as I say, not as I do," cripples quality leadership. As Ralph Waldo Emerson observed, "Who you are speaks so loudly that I cannot hear what you are saying."

3. Take an Interdependent Approach: Use All the Blocks to Build Your Pyramid

Each secret builds upon the others. Every block must be securely in place or the pyramid might crumble at the slightest tremor. The two cornerstones of the pyramid, industriousness and enthusiasm, offer a perfect example of this principle. Industriousness refers to the work ethic. There is no substitute for effort if you wish to develop your full potential as a leader and human being. Yet industriousness without enthusiasm is a painful and uninspired pursuit, leading to a feeling of tedium in which initiative and drive gradually dissipate. To access your full energy and ability, you must do what you love.

Working holistically also makes it essential to apply each principle in *every* facet of your life if you are to receive maximum value. You discover your true "golden essence" and free the leader within you when you experience the inner satisfaction of knowing you've done your best. If you seek to apply the principles only in your professional life and not in your personal, family, and spiritual life, you will not attain the sense of balance and harmony so necessary for true peace of mind. Inevitably, the stress from trying to be two different people will affect you in all areas.

Throughout the remainder of this book we will explore the secrets within each block in the Pyramid of

Success, expanding upon each element to create a personal model of leadership and inner satisfaction that opens the door to a winning life. You will emerge with a blueprint for living with remarkable balance, fulfillment, and joy in your personal, professional, family, and spiritual life. By committing yourself to consistent action as you learn the simple secrets, you will add your own contributions and discover the extraordinary leader that is inside of you.

5

Secret #1:

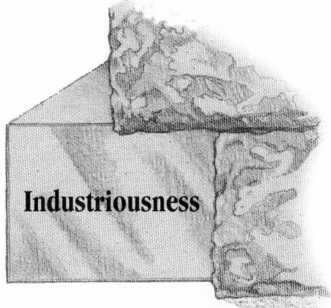

Industriousness

During the fourteen years he worked on solidifying the Pyramid of Success, Coach Wooden tried many combinations of attributes in many different locations. But the two foundational cornerstones never changed. For one he chose industriousness and for the other, enthusiasm. In his autobiography, *They Call Me Coach,* he explained succinctly and simply the importance of a solid foundation. "No building is better than its structural foundation, and no one is better than his or her mental foundation."

Perhaps it was because of his roots as an Indiana farm boy that he developed such deep respect for and belief in the importance of hard work and industriousness. There are no shortcuts on a farm. The daily demands are firm. Weeding, worming, planting, and picking must be done consistently and conscientiously. You simply cannot get away with procrastination and cramming on the farm. If you fall behind, the results are often irreversible and always painful.

The rewards for industriousness on the farm, however, are deeply satisfying. You learn responsibility and gain the self-respect that comes when you willingly accept that "If it's to be, it's up to me!" You discover the remarkable level of vitality within you when you live proactively rather than reactively. You become strong physically and emotionally because you are *doing* rather than stewing or brewing.

As a coach and leader, Wooden constantly sought to ingrain this same conviction in the importance of industriousness into all those around him. While it is true that most leaders value hard work, Coach Wooden's approach was quite unusual in several key ways. Identifying these differences is critical to fully understanding and applying the secrets of a winning life.

First of all, industriousness to Coach Wooden did not mean 16-hour days, 7 days a week, 365 days a year dedicated to one's profession. To him, industriousness must complement and not detract from a sense of balance. He placed tremendous emphasis on the importance of practice, yet ran possibly the shortest practice sessions of any major college basketball coach in the nation. All

UCLA practice sessions lasted 90 minutes. They began precisely on time, and they ended precisely on time. Despite this seemingly limited amount of practice, his teams consistently emerged as the best conditioned and most exquisitely prepared in the sport. How, then, did he manage to generate such superb results?

Industriousness must complement and not detract from a sense of balance.

The key was his understanding of an important principle about *effective* industriousness. Industriousness that creates results is a function more of focus than of time. This is not to suggest that putting in the hours to improve performance is not important. It is absolutely essential. There is no substitute. Mastering any skill or fundamental takes hours and hours of intense repetition. Yet, unless those hours are fully concentrated in the present moment, the time spent will be of little value. Coach Wooden created in his practice sessions a work environment where every moment was precious. Each drill he designed was performed at high speed and required intense concentration. There was very little idle time for any of his players. Every drill had a very specific goal or outcome. Rather than allowing his players to break between drills or to sit idly by when their unit was not involved in scrimmages, he used these transition times to work on conditioning and fundamentals. He kept practices alive with constant and purposeful movement. The overall effect was brilliant. Although the total minutes on the practice floor were minimal in comparison to other coaches' systems, the number of minutes actually sustained at high levels of physical and mental energy was extraordinarily high.

Be Prepared: Construct a Plan and Keep a Record—Then Use Them!

To create this vibrant and purposeful practice environment, Coach Wooden spent more time in design and preparation than in the practice sessions themselves. Napoleon Hill, one of the great personal development teachers of modern times, said in his classic work, *Think and Grow Rich,* "Reduce your plan to writing. The moment you complete this, you will have definitely given concrete form to the intangible desire." This focus on written preparation is a key distinction in the Wooden approach to effective industriousness. He was a meticulous record keeper, writing down statistics and notes to himself during every practice. Many leaders and managers take notes and gather information. That in itself is not unusual. What Coach Wooden did with his notes and statistics was very unusual. He actually *used* them!

Each morning he would sit down in his office and copy into his daily notebook the important information he had gathered on three-by-five cards during the previous practice. Then he would look at notebooks from previous years to examine what his prior teams had done at identical points in the season. Finally, he would spend two hours or more with his assistants, designing a plan for the upcoming practice. The planning was extremely detailed, with strict attention to making the most of every minute. Even today, Coach Wooden can pull out one of his carefully organized notebooks and tell you precisely what happened during practice at, say, 3:45 P.M. on January 26, 1953. He can tell you how well his players were shooting free throws in practice on November 20, 1969, and what specifically he felt most important to emphasize the next day.

Industriousness that creates results is a function more of focus than of time.

Application of these principles makes just as powerful a difference in the corporate arena as on the basketball floor. One of the most time-consuming and often unfulfilling activities in many businesses today is the seemingly endless barrage of meetings. There is no question that meetings create the opportunity to share information and ideas and to stimulate synergy. The challenge is that in many organizations, meetings have become unproductive infringements on people's time. Look around you at your own business meetings. What kind of energy do you see in the faces and physiology of the participants? How many of them are clearly involved and activated? Do the meetings stay on purpose, or do they seem to continually drift off on tangents? What feelings do you and the other participants walk away with after the meetings? Do you feel a sense of progress, completion, and ignition? Or do you rush back to your office filled with frustration and stress because you feel you have lost precious time and momentum?

After studying Coach Wooden's approach to practice sessions, I began to ask myself how I could create the same results in business meetings. I then identified four main elements that Wooden used in the design of his basketball practices and which could be applied in the corporate structure.

---

4 Keys to an Effective Meeting

1. **Every participant needs to be actively involved a high percentage of the time.**

2. **The meeting must start and end on time, and the clock must be used as a tool to generate energy and resourcefulness.**

3. **The meeting must produce progress; every participant must walk away with clarity about his or her next step.**

4. **The meeting must end on an upbeat note, with sincere recognition and appreciation expressed for the team's industriousness and effort.**

Using these elements as a foundation, I designed a new meeting format called the Team Possibility Workshop.

Originally, the format was used for group process teams in a Total Quality Management effort. Since that time, I have found the Team Possibility Workshop format to be extremely effective for such diverse purposes as sales meetings and strategic planning sessions.

Before I scheduled the first of these workshops, I spent considerable time preparing a detailed game plan. Right up front, I defined the key outcomes we were meeting to accomplish, and gained agreement from the team. To promote a much higher level of active participation by each person, I decided to organize the meeting into a three-step process: brainstorming, prioritization, and action commitments.

The brainstorming session was high-paced and free-flowing. We allowed no assessment of ideas during brainstorming; every idea was welcomed and recorded. In virtually every meeting some individuals fall into a group I call "dominators," and others fall into a second group I call "holder-backers." Just before we began our brainstorming session, I acknowledged the dominators (without specifically naming them, though I will admit to some pretty direct eye contact!) for being eager and enthusiastic contributors. I encouraged them to keep expressing their ideas and suggestions with their characteristic energy. I also challenged them to be as committed to helping the holder-backers step forward with their contributions as they were to offer their own.

I then shared my strong belief about holder-backers, which has been validated many times through the years. In my experience, I have often found that people who tend to hold back from expressing their ideas and opinions are exceptional observers and listeners. They take everything in and have a great deal to contribute. But, more often than not, somewhere in their past they expressed a creative or unusual idea, only to be laughed at or humiliated. They learned it was less painful to keep quiet. If we help the holder-backers feel supported and encouraged, however, they quite often come up with out-standing ideas.

People who tend to hold back from expressing their ideas and opinions are exceptional observers and listeners.

I set a relatively short time limit for the brainstorm-ing session and set them loose. The creativity and energy that filled the room amazed me. More ideas and solutions were generated in twenty minutes than in the two hours we often spent in typical meetings!

Next, we organized into new groups for the priori-tization session. Coach Wooden designed many practice drills that required varied group sizes. The variety helped keep the players fresh and stimulated. The different com-binations also built greater communication and synergy among the players. In two-on-two drills, for example, his players learned how to better support and work with specific teammates. This helped create special chemistry among his players that inevitably paid off in important game situations. I found this same strategy to be equally valuable in the Team Possibility Workshop.

During prioritization the team determined which ideas and solutions they felt to be the most important to put into action. Because everyone had participated so actively in formulating strategies during the brainstorming session, they each tended to maintain a high level of involvement during prioritization. This was now *their* meeting. They were actively involved, not merely taking up space. Each individual automatically took ownership and accepted responsibility. Again, I used the clock to keep the energy high by setting a 20-minute time frame to successfully complete prioritization. This provided the opportunity to clarify vague ideas and for individuals to champion ideas they felt had special merit. Using a simple point system, prioritization was carried out.

Finally, during the last ten minutes of the meeting, each member of the team arrived at individual commitments to action. Their heightened involvement throughout the Team Possibility Workshop added dramatically to the number of volunteers who stepped forward to tackle the key tasks for each prioritized solution.

The entire meeting lasted one hour. Our team left the meeting feeling energized, upbeat, and successful. We now use the same approach to help clients integrate our training into their organizations. The Team Possibility Workshop is an outstanding way to add value to training because it enables participants first to identify what they have learned, then to immediately activate their creativity and vitality as they decide specifically how best to use the new information.

Make Meetings More Productive with the Team Possibility Workshop

1. **Brainstorm: 20 minutes**

2. **Prioritize: 20 minutes**

3. **Commit to Action: 20 minutes**

Purposeful industriousness is characterized by two other very important distinctions. Each requires leadership that keeps the long term and the whole person clearly in view. The first, perspective, was exemplified by Coach Wooden's constant emphasis on the direct relationship between his players' non-basketball pursuits and their ultimate performance on the court. He said, "Our team condition depends on two factors: how hard you work on the floor during practice, and how well you conduct yourselves between practices. You can neither attain nor maintain proper condition without working at both."

Coach Wooden expected and demanded 90 minutes per day of intense concentration and effort from his players. During those minutes they were UCLA basketball players. If, however, they applied their utmost industriousness and enthusiasm only on the court, they would fall far short of achieving real success in other facets of their lives. Eventually their basketball would suffer as well. So Coach Wooden taught his players that when they left the practice floor, they must apply their focus and energy to being the best students, friends, and human beings of which they were capable. He wanted his players to look at themselves first not as UCLA basketball players, but rather as UCLA students who had the special privilege of playing basketball. He neither fostered nor condoned workaholism. Instead he believed in intense, concentrated, and effective work. The former eventually leads to burnout. The latter builds character and vitality.

As I work with businesses across the country, I've become increasingly aware that perhaps no problem is more prevalent and alarming than burnout. This is a challenge that demands leadership more committed to developing the best in people than to short-term profit objectives. As a leader, you must maintain a perspective that keeps balance constantly in the forefront. You must encourage focused hard work, yet discourage workaholism with equal fervor. This kind of commitment is the only way to achieve consistent long-term success. It means your team will be prepared to meet the toughest challenges with confidence, skill, and energy.

In his first fifteen years at UCLA, Coach Wooden fielded several teams he believed had the talent to win the NCAA Championship. Yet none achieved that honor. What was missing? In 1963, the year before UCLA was to begin the most successful twelve years in major college sports history, Coach Wooden searched for the answer to that question and arrived at this conclusion: "As I tried to put my finger on that one elusive factor that had stood in our way, I went back over every statistical record I had. Only one thing seemed to stand out. Perhaps I worked the players too hard early, and by season's end—or tournament time—they were too worn out to survive the rigors of that level of competition."

You must encourage focused, hard work, yet discourage workaholism with equal fervor.

Coach Wooden believed that progress occurs only through change. He made subtle adjustments to his practice schedules designed to build strength more gradually through the season. Over the next twelve years his UCLA teams went on to win ten NCAA Championships. He commented on the change this way: "Was this rather minute change the reason for our string of successes beginning in 1964? I don't know. It is the only change I made."

Even in his own life, Coach Wooden managed to keep basketball in perspective. His profession was important to him but was not the center of his life. His family, spiritual pursuits, and living according to his principles were his highest priorities. He also had the ability to focus on the present moment without dwelling on the past or drifting off into the future. This is a principle I call "being present," and it represents the final key difference in Coach Wooden's unique approach to living and teaching the quality of effective industriousness. A telephone conversation I had with him illustrated this fundamental principle of leadership.

The Difficulties and Rewards of Being Present

I had called Coach Wooden out of frustration one morning to seek his advice. I wanted to ask how he managed to maintain such balance throughout his career in the face of the intense demands his leadership and success generated from the media, alumni, university administration, and countless other sources. The evening before, I had returned home from another of what had become my typical days at the office. Driven by an unrelenting feeling of being overwhelmed, I had fallen into the habit of reaching the office by 5 A.M. and not returning home until well after 6 o'clock in the evening. As I wearily walked into the house, it was as if my body had come home, but not my mind and spirit. They were still at the office, consumed with all I had yet to complete.

My five-year-old daughter rushed to me when I opened the door, alight with excitement that her daddy was finally home. If anything could have shaken me from my obsessive intoxication with work, the pure joy and unconditional love in Kelsey's incredible hug was it. But somehow I missed it. She began to gush about all the marvelous, funny things that had happened to her that day. But I didn't really hear her. Her beautiful brown eyes lit up the room with unrestrained delight, yet my preoccupation obscured her brilliance. All I saw were deadlines, sales statistics, and unfinished projects.

As I drove to work the next day in the silence of the early morning, an intense feeling of remorse swept over me. By being so caught up in my industriousness in my career, I was losing my sense of balance. Precious moments like those I had lost with my daughter the night before could never be reclaimed.

When I related these feelings to Coach Wooden, he listened intently before responding. He exemplified a foundational principle of true leadership that Stephen Covey describes so well in *The Seven Habits of Highly Effective People:* "Seek to understand before you seek to be understood."

Coach Wooden responded to my story by saying, "First of all, realize that we are all human, and therefore imperfect. Don't strive to be perfect; just aim at being the best of which you are capable." He explained that there had been many times when it had been difficult for him, too, to be fully present for his family. But he worked as industriously at developing this ability as he did at developing his basketball teams. Through well-directed industriousness, we develop positive habits. When he arrived home each day, he immediately focused on asking his wife and children about *their* day, their challenges, and their successes. He formed the habit of listening with love and genuine interest. He focused on how important they were to him. As a result, although he sometimes had to remember to work at it, being present became more and more natural.

When you are fully present, every ounce of physical, mental, and emotional energy is keenly focused. When you think back to your most satisfying projects, activities, or interactions with others, undoubtedly your level of presence was extraordinary. Being present has an immense impact on the quality of your leadership and the level of industriousness and enthusiasm you will instill in those around you. *As a leader, nothing is more important than building trust.* And nothing is more important to building trust than being fully present for those you lead.

Through well-directed industriousness, we develop positive habits.

I once had the privilege of working with another leader who exemplified this special quality of presence. Alan Hahn remained remarkably present for his team during the most difficult time of his life. For this I will be forever grateful—not only for his leadership, but also for his example. Not long after he had been named the CEO of Robbins Research International, Inc. his son was killed in an automobile accident. Alan was devastated. It was a loss that would test the very limits of his ability to heal.

Somehow, though, Alan managed to maintain his presence in the office through this excruciating time. His door stayed open. He continued to respond quickly and thoughtfully to ideas and questions. In the midst of his great pain, it was apparent how genuinely interested he was in each of us. Even when we disagreed on a strategy or decision, I was struck by one irrefutable truth about his leadership. He was always *there*. His constant presence made a huge difference in my own confidence and dedication.

This is the power of being truly present for your team. Your teammates must develop genuine belief that you listen, that you care, and that they are important—if they are to consistently perform at their highest levels.

6

Secret #2:

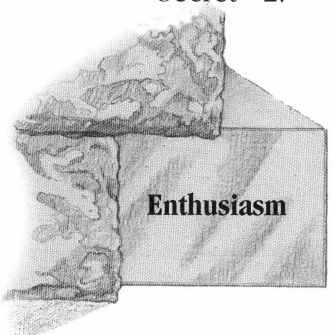

Enthusiasm

To fully achieve the best of which you're capable, you must love what you do. Industriousness and enthusiasm are inextricably bound together. *Hard work without enthusiasm leads to tedium. Enthusiasm without industriousness leads to unrealized potential. When they are present together, they cement a solid foundation leading to success.*

When I think about some of the most admirable leaders of our time—John F. Kennedy, Mahatma Gandhi,

Mother Teresa, Dr. Norman Cousins, Dr. Martin Luther King, Jr.—I recall a radiant quality, a quiet warmth and certain glow that is undeniably a product of their enthusiasm. In his brilliant work, *Gandhi: A Memoir,* William Shirer described the mahatma's light-filled presence as one that immediately uplifted those who came to see him.

> The Indians felt in the presence of the great man that something immense was suddenly happening in their drab lives, that this saintly man in his loincloth cared about them, understood their wretched plight and somehow had the power, even in the face of the rule of the great white sahibs in Delhi and the provincial capitals, to do something about it.

This kind of powerful presence is born of inexhaustible enthusiasm.

I once asked Coach Wooden what he saw as the key difference between a good team and a great team. He said that talent was important, but was not usually the key difference, as he believed that in any given season there were many teams with sufficient talent to go all the way. Year after year, he drummed into his players the three elements he felt were absolutely critical to success in basketball: condition, fundamentals, and teamwork. The team that emerged with the NCAA Championship would have the edge in these three areas. Just as with talent, however, many teams had the potential for championship-caliber conditioning, fundamentals, and teamwork. What, then, was the principal catalyst that inspired championship teams to realize their true potential?

Ultimately, it came down to one key difference in attitude. On a good or average team, the players, coaches, and managers are *willing* to work to support the team. But willingness implies a touch of reluctance, an attitude of "I'll do it, but I don't really want to." On a great team, one that comes closer to realizing the potential that God has given it, everyone is *eager* to give their best unselfishly for the good of the team. They can't wait! They are filled with the unleashing power of enthusiasm.

Take aim at three primary targets for your ever-present enthusiasm: people, fundamentals, and learning. Enthusiasm in these areas is incredibly infectious. It rubs off on everyone who comes in contact with you. You communicate your enthusiasm through your words, voice quality, and body language. Those around you sense your enthusiasm almost immediately through your physical vibrancy, whether it is the bounce in your step or the brightness in your eyes. You simply can't wait to dig into the task at hand. Enthusiasm intensifies your focus and ignites your resourcefulness.

You communicate your enthusiasm through your words, voice quality, and body language.

Perhaps no other leadership quality is more important to building a team than true enthusiasm about people. This empowers you to become a great Pygmalion. You automatically look for the best in others, their finest virtues and greatest potential. Your enthusiasm works like a magnet to draw these qualities out, helping your teammates build their confidence and performance.

Think for a moment of the people who work with you. Who seems to radiate the most constant enthusiasm? What level of activity and performance do these most enthusiastic teammates produce? For a number of years I had the great privilege of working with Raphiella Adamson, a woman who literally shined with enthusiasm. She lit up the workplace through her genuine joy at being there. When we developed a team vision statement—"We are champions of empowerment"—Raphiella put the full force of her remarkable energy behind it. She was determined to bring the vision to life, keeping it uppermost in her mind as she embraced every task she undertook, from the mundane to the extremely complex. Her vibrant spirit enabled her to view her work as an opportunity to elevate others. When she spoke with customers, vendors, or our associates around the country, she always seemed to find some special quality in them. Her enthusiasm was so overflowing, she couldn't help but share her positive observations about others with us. Over time, our entire team was affected by her enthusiasm. Raphiella had no idea how profound her impact was. Largely through her enthusiastic leadership, we forged a team that exemplified one of Coach Wooden's favorite sayings: "It's amazing what is accomplished when no one cares who gets the credit."

Discover the Fun in Fundamentals

Enthusiasm about fundamentals is the second leadership quality critical to achieving success. The greatest coaches emphasize fundamentals above all else in their practice regimens. They believe that competitive excellence often comes down to a team's ability to handle pressure. Nothing is better preparation for intense game pressure than countless hours of disciplined effort spent mastering fundamentals.

The challenge for leaders when it comes to fundamentals, however, is keeping the team focused. Your people may want to move on to more glamorous or complex challenges rather than continually applying themselves to the basics. How then, do you build an environment where attention to fundamentals is automatic and constant?

The key, once again, is your own enthusiasm as a leader. It is not enough to recognize the importance of fundamentals. Great leaders see the *fun* in fundamentals. They constantly work at helping others discover the great satisfaction that comes from mastery. Coach Wooden taught his players that basketball should be fun, not funny. To him, it is tremendous fun to develop such proficiency in fundamental skills that you abound with confidence.

No element of play was too subtle to escape Coach Wooden's notice. He believed that success usually accompanies strict attention to little details. For example, each season he taught his players precisely how to put on their socks correctly. In basketball, the feet take a terrific pounding. If their socks are slightly twisted or bunched, players are much more likely to develop blisters or soreness. The difference may be very subtle. It may take time before they notice the discomfort. But when it does occur, performance is affected.

Success usually accompanies strict attention to little details.

Coach Wooden's players were keenly aware of his personal dedication to fundamentals. When they stopped by his office to visit, they saw his notebooks in chronological order listing every drill from every practice he ever conducted. No single entry in these journals made a huge difference to the ultimate success of UCLA basketball. But the accumulation of these detailed entries, combined with Coach Wooden's fundamental practice of reexamining them and taking action, eventually did.

Progress is made through change. The challenge of change is the fear that often accompanies it. Uncertainty and doubt can work like brakes to slow our acceleration toward improvement; vibrant enthusiasm about learning can transform uncertainty into activating curiosity. Your eagerness to learn from every situation and every possible source enables you to keep your "pedal to the metal" as you drive toward growth and improvement. If people are to continually improve, perhaps no quality is more important to instill than enthusiasm for learning.

Cultivating this quality fosters a healthy drive to discover more, rather than a crippling obsession with having to be right. It builds humility and genuine self-esteem rather than an inflated, destructive ego. Don't be afraid to say, "I don't know." A challenging question can simply increase your hunger to learn and energize you with the opportunity to be exposed to new concepts and information. The mind is like a parachute—it only works when it's open! Most often, the greatest obstacle to learning the truth is the belief that you already know it.

Putting Lessons into Action: A Winning Strategy

During every off-season in his years at UCLA, Coach Wooden translated his great enthusiasm for learning into action. As soon as the final game of the season was completed, he would select a single topic that he would spend the next six months studying in extreme depth. In his early years the topic was generally a physical aspect of the game of basketball, such as rebounding or zone defenses. In later years he chose more psychological topics, such as pregame mental preparation or visualization. Throughout the off-season he devoured every piece of information he could find about his selected topic. He interviewed fellow coaches with particular strength in that area to help him identify fine distinctions that would enhance his knowledge and understanding. When he was invited to speak at coaching clinics or symposiums, he seized the opportunity to be a student and to attend as many sessions as he possibly could. Over the years, he compiled a huge journal filled with notes from these events. He often said, "It's what you learn after you know it all that counts." Even when his record had soared past any other in the history of the sport, he kept searching for more insight and information. His appetite for learning was insatiable.

It was not enough for Coach Wooden simply to study. He went much further. Since education without application is worth very little, he put his learning into action by constructing a composite of the most important distinctions he had gathered from his studies. For example, during one off-season he compiled a complete teaching volume on rebounding skills after accumulating information from a wide variety of sources. By applying his creativity to build this composite, he gained the level of insight necessary to teach effectively.

Often the best teachers are those you lead and serve. They are the agents who apply the principles and skills you teach. Their feedback is invaluable in refining and enhancing your approach. As you enthusiastically seek to learn from others, you automatically help them to develop their own leadership abilities.

It is essential to adopt the belief that people work *with* you as the leader, never *for* you. Success comes when every member of the team takes ownership of the vision and accepts responsibility for his or her part in achieving it. The greater the enthusiasm, the greater the momentum because the team is motivated by desire rather than fear. Listen carefully. Do others constantly speak of tasks and duties they *have* to do? Or do they enthusiastically bubble about things they *want* to do, *can't wait* to do, or *love* to do?

Success comes when every member of the team takes ownership of the vision and accepts responsibility for his or her part in achieving it.

We learned the words *have to* when we were little. Usually two other words were attached to give it emotional clout—*or else!* "You have to do this now or else you are going to be in big trouble." Over time, *or else* may have disappeared on the conscious level. But subconsciously, the same fear of pain, loss, or humiliation you felt as a child still rises up whenever you feel you "have to" do something. When the fear becomes severe enough, you are intensely motivated to take action. The challenge is that this motivation is generally short-lived. Sustainable motivation is not like cramming for a test. Instead it is more like constantly learning more about a subject you thoroughly enjoy.

When people talk about all the challenges they "want to," "can't wait to," or "love to" tackle, they are demonstrating the kind of unstoppable enthusiasm that leads to mastery. It is natural and automatic for them to apply their energy industriously, bit by bit and day by day, to become the best of which they are capable. Repetition becomes an exercise of choice, not of willpower.

Enthusiastic leadership may be expressed in many forms. It need not be loud or flashy. It requires only that the leader express enthusiasm through some form of consistent action. Jim Rohn, one of the finest personal-development teachers of our time, described this important principle beautifully when he said, "It's not what happens; it's what you *do* that makes the difference." When what you do is carried out with an eager spirit, the results you can create are truly staggering.

The following story of a quiet peasant from the high country in France demonstrates our almost miraculous capacity to make a difference through the awesome synergy of the Pyramid's two cornerstones, industriousness and enthusiasm.

The Impact of One Man's Unfailing Enthusiasm and Industriousness

As a young man, Elzea Bufiér owned a small farm. His life revolved around his land, his wife, and his only son. He worked hard as a farmer and was quite content with his simple, peaceful life. Tragically, he lost his boy and then his wife to sudden illnesses.

Unable to bear the thought of staying on his farm without them, he decided to search for a place of solitude. With only his dog and a small flock of twenty or so sheep to keep him company, he walked for weeks, far into the high country. Finally, he came to a spot as desolate as any in France. As he looked for a place to set up his home, he saw occasional evidence that people had once been nearby. A few scattered ruins of ancient stone dwellings, long ago deserted, dotted the barren landscape. It was in one of these ancient buildings, set off by itself, that he decided to live. The nearest village was more than two days' walk away. In complete isolation he set about his shepherding, determined to live a quiet and peaceful life.

Though deeply hurt by the loss of his family, Elzea was a good and giving man at heart. He decided that in his own quiet way, he would dedicate himself to somehow making a difference. As he looked about at the barren and desolate highlands, he formed the opinion that the land was dying from lack of trees. Only an occasional white oak stood in that forlorn landscape as far as the eye could see. He set out to remedy the bleakness of the land by planting trees.

As he herded his little flock throughout the day, he collected the acorns he found from the few sparse oaks that dotted the countryside. Each night after eating his soup, he meticulously selected the very best one hundred acorns and set them in a small pail of water. The next day he carried them with him as he walked with his sheep. For a walking stick he used an iron rod, about the circumference of his thumb and the height of his shoulder.

When he found a suitable place for the sheep to rest, he left them in the care of his dog and hiked up a little higher into the hills. There he stopped and, with great care, dug a hole with his iron rod and planted a little acorn.

In this way, each day Elzea Bufiér planted one hundred new oak trees. Beginning in the year 1910, in three years he had planted one hundred thousand trees. Of these, only twenty thousand would root and sprout. And of these twenty thousand, only half would survive and grow into tall oaks. Yet, even with this small percentage of his efforts producing the results he sought, *ten thousand* oak trees appeared where before there had been nothing.

When the First World War began, Elzea was fifty-five years old. His simple, active life had kept him strong and healthy. He was unaffected by the war, high above the fighting and destruction. He kept right on with his planting, day after day, year after year.

**Beginning in the year 1910,
in three years he had planted
one hundred thousand trees.**

In time, Elzea decided to stop herding sheep because the lambs trampled on his baby trees. Instead he began to raise bees, for they would help to spread the new and wondrous life his tireless efforts were creating.

As the war came to a close, several of the oaks now stood taller than he. On his very rare trips to the distant village for supplies, he traded his honey for beechnuts and birch seeds. He had spent so much time wandering over the land that surrounded his home that he had come to know the spots where subterranean water flowed close to the surface of the ground. He believed that beech and birch trees would flourish in these spots. He was right.

Elzea Bufiér continued his quiet planting until the day he died. For thirty-seven years he had planted at least one hundred trees each day. As his trees grew, nature amplified his miracle. The wind lifted and deposited more seeds which, in turn, drew more moisture and nourished the soil. Where once there had been only desolation, now there stood a magnificent forest with flowing streams, teeming with new life. The French Forestry Bureau set aside much of this miracle forest as protected lands. In place of the deserted ruins, new villages with children, schools, and prosperous farms sprang up. By the time Bufiér died peacefully in 1947, more than ten thousand people had moved into his forest.

Elzea Bufiér gave the world a great gift. His special brand of service was very quiet and unpretentious. He wanted no credit. But his unrelenting enthusiasm and tireless industriousness created a virtual miracle. He lived and died with the peace of mind of knowing he had given his best.

The story of Elzea Bufiér demonstrates the immense impact a single individual can create through unfailing enthusiasm and consistent industriousness. But Elzea lived and worked alone. While his solitary service to mankind was astonishing, just imagine what is possible when we engage others in our cause.

The blocks at the center of the pyramid's foundation concern our relationships with others for a very important reason. When we include others in our lives, we add strength to our own. A leader's role is to meld varied talents, styles, and experience within the organization into an unselfish, synergistic team. *As separate individuals we may be many, but when we come together as a team, we are much.* When we consistently exercise our ability to bring friendship, cooperation, and loyalty into our lives, we construct an exciting new model of possibility for the present that strengthens our hopes for the future. We build the greatest of all human creations: a true *team*.

7

Secrets #3–#5:

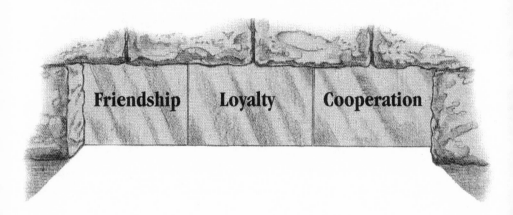

Friendship Loyalty Cooperation

A powerful, synergistic team is as attainable in the workplace as on the athletic field. As a leader, you can build principles of extraordinary teamwork into your basic culture by creating an environment where *friendship, loyalty,* and *cooperation* are conscientiously nurtured and reinforced. These three central blocks in the Pyramid of Success must become consistent priorities rather than occasional niceties if you are to master the secrets of a winning life.

Only through united effort can a team and each of its members begin to approach their true capabilities.

How, then, does a leader bring together varied talents, styles, and perspectives and merge them into a coordinated, highly productive, and deeply inspired team? Each of the three center foundational blocks plays a critical role in transforming the potential of the many into the power of one unified team.

Friendship is positioned beside industriousness because it is something we must work at constantly and diligently. It is not always easy. Many believe that friendship is simply doing nice things for others. True friendship, though, is much, much more. Often it requires courage: asking the tough question and risking a defensive or angry reaction. Sometimes, it means you continue to look for the qualities you respect in others despite their occasional failure to live up to their own standards.

An ever-present attitude of sincere friendship is one of the secrets to creating the Pygmalion spirit.

Become a "Blame Buster"

The first step in being a true friend is "blame busting." One of the most destructive and disabling symptoms of disease within an organization or a human spirit is the prevalence of blame. Like a parasite, blame latches on from the inside and begins to eat away at the spirit. When we blame others we give up our greatest strength—our own sense of responsibility. True leaders seek constantly to give credit to others and to take responsibility for giving their absolute best. They are eager to step forward and be accountable for the setbacks and difficult times because they know this will stimulate their own solution orientation while easing debilitating pressure from their team. Within this mind-set, blame simply has no place.

Blame is particularly crippling because it directs our focus to the past. Its aim is to protect egos, not to build the team. Even if blame is justified, it serves no constructive purpose. The incident is done; it's time to move on. When we are filled with a sincere attitude of friendship, our positive belief in others leads us continuously forward to solutions, not backward to blame. We see the potential to solve even the most difficult challenges because we focus on the possibility in our teammates instead of on the limitations.

Even if blame is justified, it serves no constructive purpose.

When we have instilled an attitude of friendship within ourselves and our team, we gain the ability to correct and direct constructively rather than destructively. Sincere friendship is based on mutual esteem. It allows us to constantly recognize the importance of others. It does not inhibit our ability to see specifically where we need to improve, but instead, helps us to transform problems or issues into opportunities for growth. When we identify a mistake or an area that needs improvement in people, we can help them correct their approach and behavior without tearing down their belief in themselves. It is just as important to use this constructive approach inside ourselves. Everyone benefits because we are internalizing a discipline that builds self-esteem, rather than inflicting destructive punishment that attacks a person's character. We cannot expect to have as positive an influence on others tomorrow if we have berated or antagonized them today.

When blame becomes entrenched in an organization, grudges and political fiefdoms emerge. These become insidious destroyers of momentum and divert precious energy away from the higher team vision. Focus is wasted on political positioning or crippling emotions such as jealousy, bitterness, and spite. In today's explosively accelerating business climate, it is like trying to win a drag race with the parking brake on!

John Wooden was known as a very disciplined coach. He set high standards of conduct for his players, both on and off the court. Yet, as the years went by, he had very few rules. If a player broke one of these regulations, he was disciplined and corrected, then welcomed back one hundred percent. Coach Wooden held no grudges. A fresh start was not conditional; there were no probationary periods required to earn back full status. Coach Wooden's discipline was based on respect and friendship. He looked at his players in the same way he looked at friends and family, holding high expectations for them and treating them accordingly, with dignity and respect. He never lost sight of his own fallibility and consequently was able to see mistakes as temporary errors in judgment, not permanent flaws in character. Operating from this foundation of friendship, it is easy and natural to fully forgive. Coach Wooden's players and staff responded to his humility and trust with extraordinary unselfishness and dedication of their own. Today, many years since his retirement from coaching, a remarkable number of them keep in close touch with him. It is one of the very special rewards of being a leader who refused to blame others and who constantly demonstrated sincere friendship and respect for people. He was indeed a world-class "blame buster."

Take Joy in Giving and Receiving

The second key principle at the heart of friendship centers on our ability to give—and receive—with equanimity. True leaders are not motivated to give by what they may receive in return. They give eagerly to build others up and to enjoy the peace of mind and self-satisfaction that comes from dedication to a worthy cause. Anonymous service is natural and automatic for them because they seek results, not credit. This kind of giving spirit is based on friendship and thus creates no indebtedness. Kindness and efforts to assist teammates are not tallied on some mental balance sheet; they are accepted in the same unselfish way in which they were given.

Yet great leaders are not martyrs. They happily and gratefully receive because they understand that receiving is one of the most powerful forms of giving. When we gratefully receive, we enable others to experience the same joy we feel when we give to them. It is one of the most important ways to transform ego to "we go" within our organization and ourselves.

For many in positions of leadership, it is far easier to give than to receive. That seems to come with the territory. Yet the damage we can inflict by an unwillingness to receive can deeply wound the morale and vitality within our teams.

Years ago, when I was a swimming coach, my senior kids plotted a special birthday surprise for me. They each wrote personal cards and secretly hid them along with all sorts of gifts and goodies in a meeting room behind the workout pool. Best of all, they came up with an especially creative plan for springing the big surprise. They all agreed that about halfway through the workout, one of the leaders would ask me if the team could have relays to end practice. That was their signal. As soon as I sent them off on their next drill, they all sped to the opposite end of the pool and climbed out! I stood there with my mouth open, watching them rush into the locker room en masse right in the middle of practice. I couldn't believe it. I had a mutiny on my hands!

As I look back now, I knew instinctively that the kids were up to something for my birthday. Deep in my heart, I was aware how much they wanted to show me their love and appreciation. But at the time, I couldn't handle being on the receiving end. I did not understand the importance of allowing them to give. Instead I was more concerned with control than with empowering these young people to grow.

The sad part was that I loved these kids and truly believed I was giving them everything I had to help them improve and develop as athletes and as people. In my role as coach, giving was natural. Yet I felt terribly uncomfortable when it came to receiving. I had completely missed this key component of effective leadership based on an attitude of genuine friendship.

When the kids emerged from the locker room beaming with anticipation, I exploded. I yelled at them for leaving workout without permission, telling them that "champions would never behave so irresponsibly." I even challenged their motives—suggesting they were using my birthday as an excuse for getting out of hard work. It was quite a performance. By the time I finished my tirade, I had left no survivors in the wake of my venomous wrath.

I did not understand the importance of allowing them to give.

The kids were crushed. Their excitement and glowing anticipation immediately turned to devastation and confusion. I'll never forget the pain I saw in their eyes. As I looked at their tear-stained faces I finally began to realize what hurt I had inflicted. But the damage had been done. I could not reverse the clock and start over. I had mistaken martyrdom for leadership.

Instead of providing leadership based on friendship and mutual respect, I had been blindly driven by an insatiable hunger for control. It was a very painful way to learn an essential lesson about true leadership. When we receive with genuine appreciation, we do more to empower others to develop their own leadership abilities than when we shower them with gifts and attention. A leader's ultimate goal is to develop leaders, not followers. This requires that we learn to accept recognition and praise with the same ease that we give it. By doing so, we validate each individual's belief that he or she is respected as an equal player in a total team effort.

The Ennobling Quality of Loyalty

At the center of the foundation of the Pyramid of Success we find loyalty. Without a high degree of loyalty we will fall far short of our true potential. Above all, we must be loyal to ourselves, our deepest principles and strongest convictions. Loyalty gives us the inspiration and passion to reach for the best within us, even during the most difficult of times.

Our self-respect is built on loyalty to ourselves. Being loyal means being true to our own word, refusing to compromise our values and beliefs in order to advance or gain political advantage. When we reinforce this loyalty to our own principles through words and actions, we gradually build an impenetrable fortress against procrastination and weakness. Our loyalty to our higher selves motivates us to become doers rather than stewers or brewers.

When we extend our loyalty to others or to causes we deeply believe in, we empower ourselves further to discover more of our true capabilities. One of the great truths about human beings is that we will often do more for others than we will do for ourselves. In his classic work, *Man's Search for Meaning,* Viktor Frankl poignantly expressed this fundamental importance of loyalty. In the horrifying reality of the Nazi concentration camps, dedication to others or to a special cause often meant the difference between life and death. Frankl wrote:

> I remember two cases of would-be suicide, which bore a striking similarity to each other. Both men had talked of their intentions to commit suicide. Both used the typical argument—they had nothing more to expect from life. In both cases it was a question of getting them to realize that life was still expecting something from them; something in the future was expected of them. We found, in fact, that for the one it was his child whom he adored and who was waiting for him in a foreign country. For the other it was a thing, not a person. This man was a scientist and had written a series of books which still needed to be finished. His work could not be done by anyone else, any more than another person could ever take the place of the father in his child's affections.
>
> This uniqueness and singleness which distinguishes each individual and gives a meaning to his existence has a bearing on creative work as much as it does on human love. When the impossibility of

replacing a person is realized, it allows the responsibility which a man has for his existence and its continuance to appear in all its magnitude. A man who becomes conscious of the responsibility he bears toward a human being who affectionately waits for him, or to an unfinished work, will never be able to throw away his life. He knows the 'why' for his existence, and will be able to bear almost any 'how.'

When we examine great teams in sports, business, and many other areas of life, it is clear that loyalty is a tremendous catalyst for inspired performance. For example, during my years as a swimming coach, I was constantly struck with the remarkable performances produced by athletes of all ability levels when they competed in relay events. In relays, participants feel a heightened sense of loyalty to the team. Suddenly, they know at a deep level that they are part of a bigger whole. Fueled by these feelings, they almost magically discover greater strength, speed, endurance, and concentration than they ever thought possible. We simply cannot hope to become the best of which we are capable unless we feel a strong sense of loyalty to someone or something.

Inspire Loyalty and Build Business Success

In business, inspiring genuine loyalty is becoming increasingly important if leaders are to develop people and maintain high morale in the midst of rapidly changing conditions. Technology is driving change at a dizzying pace. Where once jobs and careers were relatively stable over many decades, today whole industries are appearing and disappearing practically overnight. The brilliant economist Paul Zane Pilzer, in his best-selling book *Unlimited Wealth,* offers several powerful examples of the incredible acceleration of change through technological advances. He notes, for example, that if we turn back the clock only a few years, the personal computer was just about to be introduced, automobiles used carburetors to combine fuel and air for combustion, and the vinyl record industry was flying along at a multibillion-dollar pace. Today, the PC industry produces more than $150 billion in sales—three times the revenue generated by the big three auto manufacturers combined. Fuel injection controlled by a tiny computer chip has completely revolutionized fuel efficiency, wiping out the carburetor industry almost instantly. The compact disc has relegated vinyl records to collectors' shelves.

These are but three examples of the kinds of paradigm shifts that are occurring constantly in virtually every industry from agriculture to financial services. With the rate of change accelerating at such a remarkable pace, flexibility, learning skills, and enthusiasm for change are more critical than ever before. Your organization must be able to turn on a dime. If leaders are to build successful businesses today, they must prepare for change by instilling an abiding sense of loyalty throughout their organization. Strong feelings of loyalty sharply increase employees' eagerness to learn, grow, and flexibly adapt to change.

**With the rate of change
accelerating at such a
remarkable pace, flexibility,
learning skills, and
enthusiasm for change
are more critical than
ever before.**

Within an organization, a leader fosters loyalty by being loyal, speaking highly of people—both when they are present and when they are not—and continuing to support people when they make mistakes just as strongly as when they excel. When employees move on to other companies or careers, true leaders continue to focus on their contributions and efforts. They refuse to look at them as traitors or "bad guys." This kind of loyalty from leadership sends a great message to employees. It helps them feel important and gain confidence that their human dignity will be honored and maintained always. This, in turn, fuels their own feelings of loyalty.

During my years in the air freight industry, I saw a remarkable demonstration of the power of loyalty to transform a seemingly hopeless situation into a triumph. Our San Francisco operations manager at that time was a woman by the name of Claire Shimabukuro. Until she was assigned to this position, the San Francisco station had been ravaged by continuous conflict between operations and sales. Communication had virtually stopped between the past operations manager and the sales manager. The station survived only because of two large accounts that had been with the company for many years. New business was practically nonexistent.

When Claire arrived, she immediately established her loyalty to each individual and to the company as a whole. She steadfastly stood by people, absolutely convinced that they had all the skill, ability, and experience they needed to be successful. She refused to segregate on the basis of functional groups. To Claire, operations and sales were teammates working toward a common cause. She was intensely loyal to all her teammates, regardless of whether they moved freight in the warehouse or sold transportation services on the street.

Within thirty days of her arrival, the San Francisco office began to show signs of new life. Sales began to secure new accounts, and operations improved their customer service and on-time performance. When we called the station to discuss a challenge or project, members of each functional group joined together to find the best possible solution. The work environment became fun, friendly, and energized. Over the next year the station achieved the first consistent profitability in its history.

Claire's loyalty was as strong in tough times as in smooth times. When she assumed her new position she inherited a night operations manager who had a reputation as an extremely difficult person to work with. He was often gruff and sarcastic with warehouse employees and had antagonized several customers and vendors. He was quick to blame teammates from other locations for delivery foul-ups and had alienated many with terse and biting messages via electronic mail. Within his own station, he was respected for his knowledge, but feared and generally disliked for his sarcasm and impatience. All of us at the general office felt strongly that he needed to be replaced.

But Claire refused to give up on him. She treated him as a valued member of the team. He was exceptionally skilled at loading freight in the most economically efficient way. It was a real art, requiring the ability to visualize complex geometric combinations while calculating multiple revenue-versus-cost equations. All of this had to be done quickly and decisively. Claire spotted this special talent and acknowledged him constantly, seeking his opinions and acting on them. Gradually, he began to change. He started to instruct his teammates constructively rather than scolding them. For the first time, he sent messages of appreciation to other stations for their help in successfully handling difficult shipments. Within twelve months after Claire came to San Francisco, he was chosen by combined vote of the operations and sales managers from the entire system as the Outstanding Operations Employee of the Month. It was a remarkable transformation, resulting from unwavering loyalty.

The Value of Honoring Differences

The secret of the final block in the Pyramid's foundation is cooperation. Without cooperation, there can be no synergy. It is the combination of abilities, talents, and styles that can transform a group of individuals into a high-performance team.

One of the experiences I enjoyed as a teacher was the opportunity to work with an amazingly dedicated group of young people known as Youth for Environmental Sanity (YES). Started in 1988 by fifteen-year-old Ocean Robbins and seventeen-year-old Sol Solomon, this organization has traveled to thousands of schools throughout North America delivering the message of environmental awareness to over half a million students. As I began to train these wonderful young people in the fundamentals of team building, I was immediately struck by how diverse their backgrounds were, yet how cohesively they worked together. It was a perfect example of the students teaching the instructor!

Ocean and Sol have been able to mold these diverse individuals into a true team because they understand the value of *honoring differences.* This is the essential ingredient in successful cooperation. Within a basic framework of unselfishness and mutual support, members of YES have all been empowered to express their abilities and fulfill their roles in their own ways. Through their example, Sol and Ocean have made it clear that every member of the team is an important contributor and that ultimately their individual and collective success will be derived from the way they bring out one another's strengths.

When we learn to honor and value the differences within our teams, we vastly expand our resourcefulness. The challenge in many organizations is that leaders often view differences not as opportunities to strengthen the team, but as threats. When this occurs, cooperation and collaboration will be replaced by infighting and factionalism, with each group more concerned with having things its way than with working together for a common goal. There is a great deal of talking, very little listening, and even less action.

Solve Problems by Cultivating Cooperation

Recently, I had a special opportunity to work with another group of high school students from the Fort Worth School District. These kids had been selected to host international students from five different countries in a program called the Sister Cities Leadership Academy. Each student had been chosen because of his or her leadership abilities or potential. We spent three incredible days with these terrific young people focusing on teamwork, breaking through limiting beliefs, communication, and leadership skills. The program was highly interactive, with a great deal of our time spent in exercises and games that gave each participant an experience of the principles we were teaching.

In one of the games, the kids were blindfolded and then asked to locate a long rope, and together to form it into the shape of an isosceles triangle. Before they could remove their blindfolds, every member of the team had to be touching the rope simultaneously as they held it in the triangle shape.

Within five minutes, the kids had found the rope and formed an excellent isosceles triangle. The trouble was, they didn't realize they had already solved the challenge. Instead of trusting that their initial effort had been successful, they began to doubt each other and to vie for the leadership position. They had cooperated beautifully during the search for the rope and in their first attempt to form a triangle. However, the synergy they had created through cooperation rapidly changed to rivalry and competition for control.

At least ten different times during the next half hour they created excellent solutions, only to argue their way out of success. The lack of listening was evident because several of the kids spoke up with the same basic solution. Yet instead of following through, the participants kept repeating themselves, attempting to gain control by speaking more loudly and aggressively.

As the exercise dragged on with no end in sight (no pun intended!), some of the kids "checked out" emotionally, becoming detached and disinterested. It was a striking example of the same loss of energy and involvement that occurs within any organization when cooperation is supplanted by individual agendas.

Interestingly, the kids had learned to ask for their teammates' ideas and suggestions. Several of the most dominant and outspoken young leaders made conscious efforts to ask for input. Yet asking is not enough. Truly listening, genuinely considering, and definitively acting are required to actually cooperate. Virtually every solution the kids came up with would have worked. But they were so consumed with how they would solve the problem and with *who* would be in charge that they did nothing.

The kids learned tremendously from this exercise. They discovered that often a great leader eagerly accepts a position as a follower. This concept has been called Servant Leadership. Servant leaders are eager to do whatever it takes to support the entire team and its most important outcomes. They lead not by position or title, but instead seek to put the most qualified individual or team in charge of specific projects or campaigns. When it is appropriate for them to step forward and lead from the front, they do so without hesitation. But they are just as comfortable to let go and allow others to carry the ball.

8

Secret #6:

Self-Control

Basketball, like many sports, offers a marvelous opportunity to prepare for the many rigors and challenges of the real world. The basketball court serves as a special laboratory where coaches and players can mix various combinations and conditions to seek new and better results. Perhaps no aspect of basketball is better preparation for the responsibilities of leadership in career and family than the constant, intense pressure the game demands. Decisions must be made quickly and precisely despite an incredible amount of distraction swirling all around. At virtually every moment, someone works to deny you position and to capitalize on your slightest mistake. What's more, officials scrutinize your every move, ready to blow the whistle on any indiscretions.

Coach Wooden believed that most games were decided in the final five minutes. If the opponent proved superior in skill and talent, he could do little, if anything, about it. However, more often than not, conditioning—physical, mental, and emotional—became the critical factor during this crunch time. These were areas over which he could exercise far greater control as a coach and leader. The key to superb conditioning, he believed, was to put the sixth secret of the pyramid, *self-control,* firmly in place and at work in players' lives.

By Coach Wooden's definition, success is peace of mind, which is a direct result of self-satisfaction in knowing you've done the best of which you are capable. Without great self-control, such peace of mind is unattainable. Indeed, through diligent effort and focus, self-control gradually transforms into peace of mind as it becomes more and more automatic and natural.

One of the most important and valuable ways to develop self-control is through dedication to repetition. Most of us are too easily diverted from fundamentals. We want to add complexity before we have truly mastered the basics. But only when we control our urge for the quick fix and concentrate on repetition do we discover our true potential. Self-control and repetition must be applied holistically, in all facets of your life, if you are to achieve the transformation from deliberate, conscious focus to automatic, subconscious peace of mind. This is one of the most important reasons why Coach Wooden believed his role as a coach was to prepare young people to be successful in life first, and to win basketball games second.

Success is peace of mind, which is a direct result of self-satisfaction in knowing you've done the best of which you are capable.

Long-term thinking is fundamental to leadership. Self-control is absolutely necessary to internalize long-term thinking. As a leader, it is very important to discipline with the long term in mind. Discipline does not mean punishment, humiliation, or retaliation. The aim of discipline is to correct and improve. Discipline must be delivered calmly, firmly, and with self-control if the message is not to be lost in the messenger. Words shouted in the heat of the moment can sometimes destroy weeks and months of careful nurturing. By demonstrating self-control in the way you discipline, you signal that your goal is to correct a behavior and move forward. Your faith in the person remains strong and evident. As you exercise self-control, you are able to focus on what people do because you maintain your belief in who they *are*. Because they instinctively appreciate the difference, they respond much more positively. In this way, your example of self-control helps them to develop their own.

The Dignity of Jackie Robinson: Focusing on the Cans, Not the Can'ts

Self-control is perhaps the single most important ingredient in leading by example. One individual who exemplified remarkable self-control in the face of tremendous pressure was Jackie Robinson. When Robinson broke the color barrier in major-league baseball with the Brooklyn Dodgers in 1947, he was subjected to unbelievably intense abuse from fans, opposing players, and even his own teammates. A large and vocal segment of society wanted to prove that blacks could not make it in the big leagues, that they would crack under the emotional pressure. Their words and actions, aimed at destroying Robinson emotionally and physically, were a grim commentary on the prejudice and bias of the time.

Players on opposing teams tried to goad Robinson into fights by spitting in his face and hurling brutal epithets at him. Death threats were an everyday occurrence for Robinson in those early days. When traveling with the Dodgers, he was often refused service in restaurants and hotels, and suffered the humiliation of being separated from his peers as a so-called subhuman. Several of his own teammates sought to sabotage his success in his rookie year by psychologically and physically attacking him.

Through it all, Robinson maintained an amazing level of self-control. He was able to keep the long term in mind. He knew that if he cracked—if he snapped back in any way—it would only give ammunition to the prejudice he was working so hard to defuse. By maintaining his composure and concentrating his spirit on being the best player and teammate he was capable of being, he believed that things would work out for the best. He exercised remarkable self-control in focusing on what he could do, rather than what he could not.

When a teammate made a great play or came through with a clutch performance, Robinson was the first to acknowledge him publicly with a pat on the back or a compliment. If someone was in a slump or was feeling unsure of himself and discouraged, Robinson was there with a few words of encouragement and faith. It didn't matter if this was the same teammate who had shunned or belittled him because of his race. He saw no color, only teammates and fellow human beings.

Robinson was able to demonstrate such astonishing self-control because he had an unshakable belief in people. Faced with such prejudice and adversity, it's easy to picture him grimly gritting his teeth and hanging on with every ounce of his strength to keep from exploding. But that was not Jackie Robinson. He smiled easily and often. He was able to look past people's poor behavior and see something much better in them. He believed that it was his responsibility to be an example of dignity and self-control regardless of the odds against him. On and off the field, he controlled his focus and concentrated as well as any man who has ever played the game. He played with extraordinary intensity, using the antagonism he faced off the field to fuel his fire on it. Every ounce of his considerable energy was given unselfishly to help the team. He never campaigned to attain a position of leadership. He simply earned a leadership role because of his great character and self-control. Bit by bit, his unselfishness and class won the admiration of first his teammates, then the league, and eventually much of society.

Two Fundamentals of Self-Control

Jackie Robinson epitomizes two key facets of self-control. The first is *maintaining self-control during the toughest times,* even when the most difficult obstacles appear before you. This is when your leadership will be most severely tested. People will look to you during periods of turbulence with greater anxiety and concern than when things are sailing along smoothly. How will you handle the tough times, when short-term obstacles and fears threaten to obscure your long-term perspective? Will you isolate yourself from the team and close your doors to all but a few of your most trusted and loyal associates? Will you show signs of panic, from defensiveness to outbursts of temper? Will you try to shed responsibility by blaming others? Will you focus the organization more on what could go wrong than on what could go right? Will you stay cool and relaxed when the pressure heats up, or will you tighten up?

When you have made self-control an integral part of your leadership style, you will appear to thrive under pressure. This is because you will view problems and obstacles as challenges and opportunities that enhance your ability to discover greater resourcefulness in yourself and your team. Leading with a high degree of self-control does not require that you stifle your spirit and vitality. It simply means that you direct your energy productively, toward what you most want to be and do as a leader.

Leading with a high degree of self-control does not require that you stifle your spirit and vitality.

When you respond to adversity with calm assurance and even greater faith in people than they sometimes have in themselves, they are much more likely to rise to the occasion and make decisions with confidence and enthusiasm. They will mirror your self-control and assurance as they work with customers, fellow employees, and vendors. Ultimately, you will instill a belief in your organization that short-term downturns and obstacles are no match for your team's long-term ability to successfully tackle any challenge.

Jackie Robinson also provided us with a brilliant example of the second key facet of self-control—*patiently sticking to your own game.* On the base paths, he kept coming with relentless aggressiveness. If he was thrown out trying to steal home, everyone in the ballpark knew he would explode for home plate the next chance he had, with even more determination and intensity. Even when his legs were shredded by the sharpened spikes of opponents trying to weaken his resolve, Robinson controlled his fury and waited for the next opportunity to steal a key base or score the pivotal run.

Off the field, sticking to his own game meant that he would answer even his most ardent critics with courtesy and intelligence. He refused to bad-mouth anyone, choosing instead to focus on what he could respect in others. He was an articulate, sincere, and caring human being, and held himself to his own high standards of decency and team play regardless of the despicable treatment he often received. He played the game of baseball and the game of life *his* way.

Ultimately, this aspect of Robinson's remarkable self-control had the most profound impact on others. He became as revered for his leadership and human dignity as for his great baseball accomplishments. He earned the respect and adulation of blacks and whites alike. By sticking to his own game, he made a lasting difference for all of us.

As you use the fifteen secrets to develop your leadership potential, one final element of self-control will play a pivotal role in your overall success. Ice hockey legend Wayne Gretzky once said, "You miss 100 percent of the shots you never take." The same is true of your efforts to stretch and grow in each block of the pyramid. You cannot control outcomes, but you can affect them. As you seek to become the best of which you are capable, you will undoubtedly make mistakes and take wrong turns. You will be severely tested by rejection, doubt, overwhelm, and fear. At times you will feel you've given all you have to give and have still fallen short of realizing your aspirations. But, as long as you decide to keep playing the game, you control one of the most important ingredients in ultimate success. This is your absolute determination never to quit.

Scaling the Summit:
The Drive to Keep Going

Recently I heard a remarkable story from a great mountain climber named Yves Laforest, which brought this crowning element of self-control into clear perspective. Yves told the story shortly after his return from a successful attempt to reach the top of Mount Everest.

He had spent over five years preparing for his dream of reaching the highest point on the planet, more than 29,000 feet above sea level. The obstacles facing a team of climbers attempting this extraordinary challenge are almost beyond belief.

The climbers must build four camps between 17,000 feet and 26,000 feet before the actual ascent to the peak can be attempted. When they have finished setting up each camp, the climbers must return to base camp to replenish their precious supplies of food, shelter, and oxygen. Thus, they move up and down the mountain not once, but four times before they are in a position even to consider a final ascent. This demands several weeks of slow, grueling effort. Weather is a constant nemesis. The icy winds can become so fierce that the climbers must burrow into their tiny shelters and hang on helplessly, sometimes for days, until a gale subsides enough that they can inch forward once again.

Breathing at heights above 20,000 feet is astonishingly difficult. Imagine trying to breathe after running up fifty flights of stairs as fast as you possibly can. Your lungs would scream as you gasped for precious oxygen. That is how it feels to breathe *at rest* when you are above 20,000 feet.

The final camp at 26,000 feet is called "Death Camp" by the climbers. The dead bodies of two Sherpa guides, frozen solid, lie eerily on the ice. There they remain as constant reminders of the tenuousness of life at 26,000 feet. There is no way to bring the bodies down because every last reserve of energy and oxygen must be conserved to safely return the living. When the adventurers finally reach this camp they wait, often for days, for a rare crack in the weather when visibility and conditions allow for an attempt at the summit. The climbers must be prepared twenty-four hours a day to seize the slightest window of opportunity whenever it comes. Thus, sleep is fitful at best, with exhaustion creeping into every cell of their oxygen-starved bodies.

After two and a half days spent silently enduring the maddening whiteout that surrounded them, Yves's party decided that they could wait no longer than twelve more hours for the weather to improve before they would have to return to the lower camps for oxygen and supplies. At four o'clock in the morning, the break they had been praying for came. For the first time since they had reached Death Camp, looming before them they could see their obsession, the face and pinnacle of the mighty Everest.

Yves and one of his teammates were the first to gather the strength to attempt the final ascent. Balanced precariously between the adrenaline boost of closing in on their dream and the nearly total exhaustion brought on by oxygen deprivation, they inched up toward the summit. As they neared the top, the power of their spirits grew stronger. In the last few hundred yards the pain and exhaustion were temporarily forgotten, vanquished for the moment by exhilaration and triumph. Finally, after nearly a decade of training and preparation, they stood together at the very top of the world. It was a moment they would cherish for the rest of their lives.

Balanced precariously between the adrenaline boost of closing in on their dream and the nearly total exhaustion brought on by oxygen deprivation, they inched up toward the summit.

Although the ascent is the most demanding and exhausting phase of the expedition, the descent is the most treacherous. On the way up, each step is cautious and deliberate. Alertness is heightened, with every ounce of concentration focused on attaining the summit. But once the goal has been reached, a natural, subconscious letdown often occurs. The dream has now become a reality. It is on the way down that more climbers are lost, because when that razor-sharp edge is dulled, one moment of carelessness can be fatal.

As Yves and his partner made their way down from the summit, they willed themselves to hold their focus. After nearly an hour of slow and careful descent they passed two more teammates, who were closing in on the final stage of their attempt at the peak. Very few words were exchanged as all sought to conserve precious energy, but the signs of triumph and satisfaction communicated by their faces bolstered their weary companions, recharging them for the last stage of their ascent.

After nearly an hour of slow and careful descent they passed two more teammates, who were closing in on the final stage of their attempt at the peak.

Nearly a week later Yves learned of the amazing hours that followed this chance meeting with these teammates. They too had reveled in their moment of achievement atop the mightiest mountain on the face of the earth. As they began their descent, the blessed crack in the weather that had opened their window of opportunity closed abruptly, and they found themselves in the midst of total whiteout. Exhausted and running low on oxygen, they became separated. One of the climbers managed somehow to make it back to camp. But his partner found himself completely lost. Radio contact was worthless because without improvement in the weather, a search party could not be launched.

Desperately fighting to control the rising panic that threatened to paralyze his spirit, the lone climber teetered on the very brink of life and death. His only hope was to keep moving forward. He knew that if he gave up and stopped his search for camp, he would last only minutes before the intense cold would swallow him and he would die, frostbitten and starved of oxygen. Yet the temptation to simply give in to fatigue and hopelessness was nearly overwhelming.

Finally, he could bear no more. But just as he was about to sit down and give up his life, a gust of wind opened a small seam of light through the previously impenetrable whiteness. There, no more than one hundred yards in front of him, was the lifesaving sanctuary of Death Camp. Minutes later he was safely back in the shelter of his tent.

Living beyond success is a product less of talent than of tenacity. Just like the climber, you may be closing in on your dreams at the very moment when you think they are all but lost. To develop the legendary leader inside of you, you must be continually eager to take another step in the direction of your dreams. No matter how difficult circumstances may appear, remember, no one can make you give up or give you the drive to keep going. That is your decision alone. You control your own hope.

9

Secret #7:

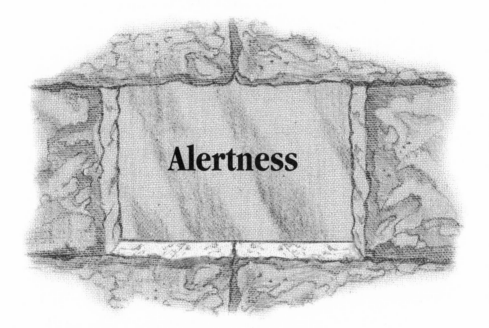

Alertness

One of the many fun and revealing exercises we conduct in our leadership and team-building seminars is called the "Blind Date." Each participant is given a blindfold and asked to find a buddy for this fascinating little adventure. During the Blind Date, participants are blindfolded for half the session and serve as seeing-eye guides for their partners during the other half. Before we send the couples off to explore, we give the guides three simple instructions:

See the World with New Eyes

1. **Help your Blind Date discover more of the world than he or she ever would have with eyes open.**
2. **Make the experience incredibly fun, creative, and stimulating.**
3. **Take great care of your partner!**

It always creates quite a stir in a hotel or conference center when I set these "odd couples" loose around the building. Off they go, groping about tentatively with one hand while with the other they hang on to their guides for dear life. Gradually they begin to relax their grip and trust their guides more completely. As they let go of their fear and doubt, a remarkable transition occurs. They discover the seventh secret of the Pyramid of Success, an *alertness* that adds unimagined richness to their experience.

As the exercise progresses, their other senses seem to come to life, and they become aware of so much more around them than they had previously noticed. Leaves that had been inconsequential green shapes suddenly become fascinating mini-ecosystems with varied textures, distinctive odors, and a cool and soothing feel between the fingers or against the cheek. Participants sense when others are nearby, even when they are silent and still. That awareness provides them with a wonderful metaphor for the deep, spiritual connection we have to other human beings.

When we reconvene to talk about the Blind Date, participants marvel at how many new thoughts and realizations they discovered from this surprising experience. An unexpected "aha" is how much more alert and aware of the world around them they became not only when they were blindfolded, but also when they served as guides. By taking responsibility to enrich others' experience, we cannot help but enrich our own. This is one of the hidden gifts of leadership. As we accept accountability for assisting people to discover their true potential, we automatically and dramatically increase our own alertness.

Alertness plays a huge role in our ability to be effective leaders because it sharply increases the raw material we make available to ourselves to enhance creativity and generate solutions. As we become more alert to what people are doing, we gain valuable insight into what beliefs are driving their actions. By understanding their beliefs, we are far better prepared to coach them when they are struggling. We can then help them make changes that will create a lasting positive difference by attacking root causes rather than alleviating temporary symptoms.

Sharpen Your Powers of Observation

By improving our alertness, we dramatically increase our opportunities to learn from those around us. When I was a senior at Stanford University, I enrolled in a developmental psychology course that made me keenly aware of how rarely most of us cultivate our powers of observation. The class was called Observation of Children. It was held once a week for three hours at a preschool located on the Stanford campus. Each of us selected a different child to be our subject for eleven weeks. Our task was to observe everything we possibly could about the child during our three hours each week. At the end of the eleven weeks, we were to prepare a paper detailing all we had observed and learned from the experience. We were not allowed to speak to our subjects, and were instructed to try to be as invisible as possible. The children at the preschool were accustomed to having Stanford students around constantly, so it was easy to blend in. I remember thinking to myself as I bicycled to the first session that this was going to get boring pretty fast. How much was there to learn by watching a four-year-old child for three straight hours?

Within minutes I found out how wrong my prediction had been. I was completely captivated. It became immediately obvious to me that I had never really focused 100 percent of my concentration on observing anyone just "being themselves" for more than about a minute and a half! About the closest I had ever come was when I had attended a play or a movie. But I soon found this true-to-life theater far more fascinating. The hours flew by. I emerged with pages and pages of detailed notes and an "I can't wait till next week" attitude.

Over the course of the next ten weeks I found myself feeling incredibly connected to the little girl I had chosen (coincidentally, her name was Allison), although I had never spoken a word to her. I knew that she was aware I was her observer, from her occasional smile or backward glance to see if I was paying attention. She was an Australian child, and each week I noticed her language becoming more Americanized from interaction with the other children. She had a delightful smile and an imagination that knew no bounds. I could see how brightly she lit up when she received a word of praise or a look of encouragement from one of the teachers or staff. I wondered if they had any idea how important their interaction with her really was. It occurred to me how much more effective and on target they could be as teachers if they were to take even fifteen minutes to step into my observer shoes.

The Importance of Sensitivity and Asking Questions

In business and coaching, I have always remembered the lesson I learned from my experience in Observation of Children. Whenever possible, I seize the opportunity simply to watch and listen to those around me. I often learn more in a few minutes of acute observation or in five minutes of uninterrupted listening than in a month of busily going about my work, shuffling papers, talking on the phone, or giving instructions. The insights I gain from these moments of quiet observation are invaluable in working more closely with people. It is equally true at home with my wife and children. I become infinitely more alert to what is important to each individual, so that I can serve that person better as a husband, father, teammate, or coach.

Developing a keen sense of alertness is a fundamental goal of all great leaders. Mahatma Gandhi set aside each Monday as a day of silence. During these silent hours Gandhi sharpened all his powers of observation, awakening his deeper listening skills and strengthening the connection he made with others through his *darshan,* or presence.

As you might imagine, Coach Wooden was also a master of observation. He rarely held chalk talks or team meetings during practice sessions. Instead, his players were in constant motion, performing high-speed drills orchestrated like a symphony. Most of Wooden's time was spent on observation and clear, succinct instruction. When he spotted something that needed correction, he was very direct. He wasted few words, choosing instead to quickly point out the error and to describe the proper behavior very specifically.

Constant observation helps you to become very sensitive and alert to the best way to work with each individual. Great leaders do not believe in treating each person exactly the same. Some of those around you respond best to praise, while others need to be pushed harder. Still others excel when they are given space with only an occasional comment or acknowledgment. This kind of individualized coaching and leadership demands a higher level of alertness, understanding, and presence. The reward is the immense internal satisfaction of seeing those around you grow in confidence and performance.

We can markedly increase our alertness through two key decisions. First, we must decide that learning is far more important than our fear of failure. This will get us off the bench and into the game. It frees us to seek to understand, to learn, and to care. We will be far more interested in *asking questions* and *listening* to expand our knowledge and deepen our insights than in spouting answers to impress others with our position or protect our frail ego. Through this first critical decision, we will become curious rather than closed, vibrant rather than stagnant.

We often get caught up in believing our primary role is to supply answers. True leaders realize that answers are important, but questions are *essential*. When you ask more questions, you gain the opportunity to see different perspectives and approaches. This enables you to be alert to opportunities or potential problems you may have missed had you confined yourself solely to your own range of experiences.

Other people benefit just as much when you remember to ask as well as tell. They see that you value their thoughts and opinions. This builds far greater loyalty and enthusiasm than if you try to force their commitment through your authority. In fact, by genuinely listening to those who question your leadership, you can often transform their doubts into lasting respect and gain valuable insights for yourself as well.

A Valuable Exercise in Listening

I experienced the transformative power of truly listening when I was asked to replace the vice president/general manager of a franchise company in the personal development industry. Almost immediately after accepting the job, I sensed that one of my key assistants was having a very hard time with the change. She had been unfailingly loyal to my predecessor, a seasoned veteran in franchising and a man of great integrity and knowledge. She was terribly disappointed that he was no longer with the company and was deeply concerned that the organization would suffer with a relative upstart like me thrust into the leadership position.

I very much wanted to set our relationship on a positive track because she was exceptionally talented and invaluable to the organization. She had earned the trust and respect of the franchisees as an extraordinary resource. Yet, despite my efforts to break down the barriers, I could feel her resistance to my leadership whenever we were together. I was having a difficult time trying to figure out how to earn her trust. Without her full support, moving this young company forward would be a huge uphill battle.

After giving her some extra space for a few days, I finally asked if we could get together and talk. When she arrived, I could immediately sense her discomfort. I told her she was very important to the organization and to me, and that my purpose in asking her to come in was to listen to her so we could learn to work together. I told her I knew this was a tough time for her, and that I very much wanted to know more about her because everyone in the company held her in such high regard. Then I asked if she would be willing to try a method of communicating that my wife and I used from time to time when we really wanted to listen to one another. The idea was very simple. For ten minutes or so, she would say whatever she wanted to say, without any interruption. My whole purpose would be to listen and to be completely present for her. When she finished, I would have my turn to speak.

She said she didn't know if she would have much to say, but would give it a try. She started slowly, but soon the floodgates opened! For the next hour I listened to her hopes, her fears, her frustrations, and her delights. I didn't say a word. I simply listened without formulating what I would say in response. When she finished, she was bright and vibrant. Somehow, my listening had communicated how much I truly cared far more clearly than any words I could have spoken. When it was my turn to speak, she listened with equal intensity. Because I had listened to her, she wanted to listen to me. We left with an entirely new relationship based on mutual respect and genuine eagerness to work together toward common goals. The relationship continued to grow through the years. Seeking to learn and understand made all the difference.

When you ask rather than tell, you not only sharpen your own alertness, you also increase others' as well, because you enable them to discover their own solutions instead of merely carrying out yours. Abraham Lincoln once said, "The worst thing you can do for those you love is to do the things they could and should do for themselves." When you ask questions of your people, you *em*power rather than *over*power. You will create leaders ready and eager to make decisions.

Activate Your Mental Resources by Defining What You Want

Besides deciding that learning is more important than our fear of failure, there is another key decision we must make to improve our alertness: we must *define specifically what we want.* When we know precisely what it is that we want, we immediately become dramatically more alert to what can assist us.

This seemingly magical phenomenon is actually a physical reality. Each of us has a netlike group of cells at the base of the brain called the reticular activating system, or RAS. This network of cells acts as the brain's filter to keep out unnecessary stimuli. Lou Tice, a noted personal development educator, calls the RAS the brain's "executive secretary." It keeps out the "junk mail" and "screens all calls."

Without an effective RAS, we'd go stark-raving mad. There is so much stimuli bombarding us that without an efficiently functioning RAS, we would experience a massive sensory overload. If you've ever had an ant crawl up your leg, you've felt your RAS spring into action. As you flick the ant off your leg, suddenly you notice little itches all over your body! Every one of your hair and skin cells contains nerve receptors that send messages to your brain. When you noticed that single little ant on your leg, you warned your RAS to be on the lookout for more of the same kind of itchy activity. Thus alerted, your RAS lets in far more stimuli than usual. You find yourself scratching and wiggling all over as if that ant had invited its whole colony to join in the fun!

The RAS appears to admit only two key types of information: that of immediate value, and that which is a threat. When we define specifically what we want, it is as if we flip a switch, activating the RAS. Information that was always available to us suddenly has value, and we notice it as if it were brand-new.

Zeroing in on the Trip of a Lifetime

During my years in the air freight industry, I had the privilege of working with a woman named Vivian who told me of an experience that demonstrated the incredible importance of the RAS. An outstanding customer service representative in Houston, Vivian was perhaps the most organized individual I have ever met. Her files were perfectly labeled and ordered, and her desk meticulously maintained. She seemed to be prepared for virtually any challenge. Once, I visited the Houston station to conduct an off-site training. As I handed out the written materials for the day, we discovered that they were shrink-wrapped so tightly, it was very difficult to remove the plastic. Without batting an eye, Vivian reached into her purse and pulled out a pair of scissors. Our problem was solved. She was amazing!

In her late thirties, Vivian became afflicted with multiple sclerosis. She was truly an inspiration to her co-workers because of the way she battled the disease. Nothing could dampen her spirit and determination to live a normal life. Sometimes the MS flared into serious episodes, forcing her to be hospitalized for several days. As soon as she could, Vivian hustled back to work, focusing on serving her customers and doing her job to the best of her ability. She refused to let the disease overpower her spirit.

The pride and joy of both Vivian and her husband was their sixteen-year-old daughter. She was an excellent student, involved in all sorts of extracurricular activities. Just before Christmas break during her junior year in high school, she rushed home filled with excitement. Beaming, she told her parents that she was one of only thirty students selected from the state of Texas to participate in an international leadership program. She would have the opportunity to travel to Europe for one full month and live with families in four different countries! She was so animated and so completely delighted that Vivian and her husband were thrilled for her and immediately told her how proud they felt.

The next day, their daughter brought home a package of information about the program. In their excitement and enthusiasm, they had assumed that the trip would be funded by the state school system. But as they read the information, a painful reality set in. The trip would cost Vivian and her husband almost $7,000! They simply did not have the money. Vivian's medical bills had completely drained their savings and they were living paycheck to paycheck, barely able to cover expenses. The two parents sat down together, knowing rationally that there was no way they could come up with $7,000 by the February 1 due date. For just a moment they agonized over how they would break the painful news to their daughter. Then, almost as one, they remembered the unabashed joy in her eyes and made a seemingly irrational decision. She was going! They had no idea how they would pull it off, but somehow their daughter was going to be on that plane!

In that moment of decision, they had defined very specifically what they wanted. Automatically, they both activated the RAS.

A couple of days later, Vivian went up to her attic to retrieve some Christmas presents she had hidden there. As she opened an old file cabinet where she kept extra greeting cards, one of the other files caught her eye. Remember, Vivian was so incredibly organized she knew where virtually every piece of paper she owned was stored. Yet, until her RAS was turned on by the prospect of her daughter's trip, she had paid no attention to this file, marked *Term Insurance.* Now, something clicked in her mind. She pulled out the file and began to read the fine print of a heretofore forgotten insurance policy. Suddenly she let out a shriek of joy and bounded downstairs. The policy could be cashed in for $5,000! It had been gathering dust in her attic until her RAS was activated by the incredible value she placed on her daughter's happiness.

Vivian's medical bills had completely drained their savings and they were living paycheck to paycheck, barely able to cover expenses.

She was so excited that she immediately wrote cards to several friends and family members to tell them the amazing story. She still had no idea how she would come up with the additional $2,000, but she was even more certain now that she would find a way.

About a week after sending off the cards, another miracle occurred. Donations, some from people she didn't even know, began to stream in. Her story had so touched and inspired her friends that they in turn told their friends, who told their friends, and on and on. Within two weeks, they received more than $3,000 in gifts for their daughter! She was on that plane to Europe, and enjoyed the experience of a lifetime.

Donations, some from people she didn't even know, began to stream in.

When Vivian related this story to me, her eyes filled with tears of appreciation and joy. She had never known that people could care so much and give so willingly. Yet she and her husband truly deserved the greatest thanks. Their decision defined precisely what they wanted and ignited their RAS. Their heightened alertness enabled them to discover information, resources, and synergy they hadn't known existed.

Intensify Your Vision—Focus on Solutions

Understanding the RAS can make an immense difference in your ability to build your team and bring out the very best in people. The key is to proactively create a clear vision of what you want for your organization and for each individual under your supervision. The more vivid the vision, the more powerfully your RAS will function. When you combine self-control with this enhanced alertness, you will be able to assess more clearly and effectively the increased information and resources you receive. You will be more alert to possibilities and better prepared to act on them intelligently and decisively.

An unexpected setback or problem will also set off the RAS. Again, you will be alerted to information and resources that otherwise might have gone unnoticed. In this case, however, you have not proactively defined what you want. Instead, you have reacted aggressively to what you don't want. When your RAS is fueled by desperation rather than inspiration, it is more difficult to support your heightened alertness with self-control. You may distort or magnify information out of proportion because of a sense of time urgency or panic, and make decisions driven more by fear of negative consequences than by positive expectations of what you truly want. When this occurs, you may cut yourself off from new and better possibilities because you feel you *must* act on the first option that comes along.

That is why it is so critical to respond to setbacks and problems by rapidly redirecting your focus to the outcome you truly desire. You must first clearly and objectively observe the problem. You cannot learn anything if you pretend the problem does not exist. But, if you become fixated on what you don't want, your RAS will efficiently kick in, speeding all sorts of information to support your fears. A wonderful question that automatically shifts your focus from problem to solution is, "What's our true, desired outcome?" When you use this question to shift your vision from the obstacles that block you to what you really want, you hold the key to transforming problems into opportunities.

A wonderful question that automatically shifts your focus from problem to solution is, "What's our true, desired outcome?"

A perfect example of this shift from obstacle to desired outcome occurred during my years with Lynden Air Freight. When the price of oil plummeted in the mid-1980s, our primary market—service between the domestic U.S. and Alaska—slowed to a trickle practically overnight. Nearly 75 percent of our company's volume was generated from the oil construction industry in Alaska, a highly specialized niche. For a short time, we felt paralyzed. Our focus was directed so strongly toward the Alaskan market that initially we felt our only alternative was to cut back sharply through layoffs and pay cuts. During this difficult period, we did not ask ourselves specifically what we truly wanted. Instead, we found ourselves clinging to the faint hope that the price of oil would somehow rise enough that Alaskan construction would resume and we could return to business as usual.

The president of the company did not allow us to remain in this state of paralysis for long. He asked us to define more clearly what we truly wanted. By simply asking, "What's our desired outcome?" a dramatic shift was set in motion. We saw that we did not want to return to the past. Instead, we wanted to become a more diversified company, noted for outstanding service, and capable of consistent and profitable growth. We wanted to provide outstanding opportunities for career advancement within the organization, and to sharply increase our productivity standards. By conceiving a more vivid vision of who we wanted to be, we suddenly became far more alert to the many opportunities that were readily available.

Within a very short time, we established ourselves as a strong player in the Hawaiian air freight market and nearly doubled our domestic U.S. business. We found that many of the special skills we had developed in serving an inbound market like Alaska (where more goods are imported than exported) gave us a similar edge in the Hawaiian marketplace. By directing our focus toward a specific definition of what we wanted to become, we reactivated our organizational energy. Once again, we were growing, improving, and increasingly alert to new possibilities.

There are times, however, when our alertness will be challenged even though we have ignited our RAS by clearly defining our desired outcomes. We may decide precisely what changes we want to make in ourselves or our team, and begin taking aggressive action to achieve those improvements, yet receive no perceptible evidence to reinforce our vision. In fact, we may be given well-intentioned information or advice that discourages us from raising our hopes or seeking to change and grow. At these times we must become increasingly alert not to external signs, but rather to the integrity of our own internal motivations. We must allow our faith to become a bridge that will keep us connected to possibility, until that faith is validated by tangible proof.

A remarkable story of one family's love, perseverance, and faith demonstrates the importance of remaining alert to possibility despite seemingly impossible odds. With each day a frightening realization loomed larger for Barry Kaufman and his wife, Samahria: One of their six children was not developing normally. All day long the boy spun nonsensically in circles, never speaking, completely divorced from contact with others. The doctors delivered their diagnosis with painful finality. The Kaufmans were told that their son was afflicted with autism, an incurable illness. The prognosis offered not even the tiniest glimmer of hope. In his powerful book, *Son Rise: The Miracle Continues,* Barry Neil Kaufman describes the empty future doctors foresaw for his son:

> At best, they insisted, the outcome would still be a severely dysfunctional human being requiring custodial care. They didn't want us to delude ourselves with unrealistic hopes. We disagreed. Hope, we knew, kept us alive and fueled our program. We knew we had no guarantees; in fact, we knew we were playing the longest of long shots.

Imagine the despair most of us would feel if we received such a hopeless prediction from qualified specialists about someone we love. We afford special respect to those we consider experts, subconsciously sanctifying them as "who-saids" of the greatest magnitude. When they speak, we listen. Often their advice is tremendously valuable, protecting us from harm and enhancing our understanding, confidence, and spirit. As children, our parents are "who-saids." Later we elevate our teachers, coaches, doctors, and heroes from the sports or entertainment worlds to this position of extraordinary influence. The confidence we place in who-saids enables them to define our direction and even determine the input our RAS seeks out. But, like all Pygmalions, who-saids can be positive or negative. We can allow their words to become a kind of life sentence without the possibility of parole, or a coronation of newfound confidence and hope. The choice is ours.

Despite the bleak pronouncements of the experts, the Kaufman family refused to accept this dismal prognosis. They made an extraordinary decision to lead rather than follow—to create possibility when others saw only hopelessness. Barry Kaufman later wrote:

> No matter how the world might label my son different, handicapped, or retarded, I wanted to stay in touch with his beauty, his singularity, his daring, and his accomplishments. When physicians, family, and friends deemed him terrible and tragic, Samahria and I created a different vision, seeing in him a child of beauty and wonder. I knew

our son was neither terrible and tragic nor beautiful and wonderful. Those words reflected beliefs—what we chose to make up about the little boy we saw. I really liked the vision we had created; it brought us happiness and hope and freed us to try for more when others counseled us to turn away.

The Kaufman family demonstrated such indefatigable determination, fortitude, and love that they created a seemingly miraculous transformation. They realized that they would have condemned themselves just as hopelessly as their son, had they not chosen to step forward and lead despite the odds. By first embracing the possibility of profound and lasting change where others saw only hopelessness, the Kaufmans kindled within themselves the spark of a new vision for their son. Then, bit by bit, their daily actions in the direction of this vision began to redefine previous limits, increasing their alertness to the tiniest signs of hope, and eventually creating results of striking proportion. Through their unshakable resolve they brought out the best in this young boy, breaking through immense barriers of belief and transforming the impossible into a stunning new reality. Today, Raun flourishes and the Kaufmans' Options Institute helps other families around the world to reach their so-called unreachable children. In the foreword to his father's book, Raun related the everyday facts of his miracle:

So I bet you're wondering what this product of "false hope" is doing with his life lately. Well, I'm enjoying college (I'm in my sophomore year) more than any other period of my life. I'm having a thoroughly terrific time choosing my own courses, living away from home, eating school food (yum!). I take courses like philosophy, political science, theater arts, and biology. I took calculus during my freshman year. Definitely not my calling. In addition to enjoying the social and academic scenes at college, I'm also on the debating team, I take ballroom dancing, I'm in a coed fraternity, and I'm in a number of political groups. I recently cast my first presidential vote after working for my candidate's campaign. (I won't say who I voted for, but you can probably guess.)

. . . What turned it around was not a string of events, but rather a wildly different and unheard of perspective: Refusing to accept the age-old view of autism as a terrible catastrophe, my parents came up with the radical idea that my autism was a chance—a great opportunity, in fact—to try to reach a child lost behind a thick, hazy cloud. It was a chance to make greatness out of something commonly viewed as unquestionably sad and tragic. This perspective, combined with a passionate relentlessness on the part of my parents, enabled me to undergo a spectacular matamorphosis and emerge from the shell of my autism without a trace of my former condition.

The Kaufman family's story of perseverance and unconditional love illuminates the single greatest challenge to sustained personal and team growth. Often people can be tricked into giving up on their dreams because they don't see significant progress right away. In the first several months of working with young Raun, his minute improvements were invisible to the family. With no feedback to support their plan it would have been easy to give up hope. They had no models to emulate, no evidence to buoy their spirits in the face of the apparent lack of progress. But their faith was inexhaustible. Eventually the tiny, imperceptible advances grew into small but noticeable steps.

With most of us, becoming alert to our own *internal* changes can be equally difficult to recognize, because they, too, are usually very subtle and inconspicuous. But the process of personal growth is similar to physical growth. When I look at my two young daughters I sometimes catch myself thinking, "Are these children ever going to grow?" I am with them so consistently each day that I don't notice the miraculous changes that are actually occurring. My alertness to their development becomes desensitized because their growth is so gradual and incremental. But then their grandmother visits after not seeing the girls for a year and exclaims, "My goodness! Look how much you've both grown!" Or one evening we'll break out our family photo albums and suddenly be jolted into realization when we see just how dramatic the change in our children really is. I call this *snapshot shock.*

Just as children grow moment by moment in tiny, continuous increments, the same process of development and change is possible inside of you emotionally, spiritually, and mentally. The secret is to maintain the same absolute conviction about your potential for personal growth that you have about the inevitability of your children's physical development. As you begin to use the fifteen secrets actively in your life, occasionally you may find yourself in a situation that startles you with that same snapshot shock revelation. You will surprise yourself by leading where you once would have followed, or by remaining poised and confident in a situation that once would have left you frightened and filled with doubt. But more often than not, the changes will be much less obvious. In these times when progress seems to have slowed to a standstill, it is your unyielding belief in possibility and your irrepressible alertness that will carry you through.

10

Secret #8:

Initiative

Some time ago, a writer with a long and successful career built a magnificent home on the coast of Oregon. It was his ritual each morning to rise before the sun and climb the winding staircase to his studio that faced the beach. There he would sit, gazing out of a huge picture window, silently drawing inspiration from the ever-changing wonder of the sunrise. Enriched by the beauty and serenity, he would then begin to write.

One morning the writer awoke as usual, headed upstairs, and began his quiet meditation. The sun was just coming up and a soft mist hung over the shore. As he gazed out at the beach, he was transfixed by what looked like a mystical dance, far off in the distance. He found himself completely fascinated as he tried to make out what it was; soon he could think of nothing else. After a short time his curiosity overpowered him; he simply had to know what it was. He put on his coat and began to walk down the beach toward the mysterious figure.

As he drew nearer he could see that the "dancer" was a young girl, around eleven or twelve years old. Again and again she bent down to grasp something from the sand, then ran out into the waves. She moved gracefully and purposefully. When the writer drew very close, he realized what she was doing. One by one, she was throwing starfish into the sea.

As the writer looked down the beach, he saw that thousands of these beautiful creatures had been washed up on the shore. He approached the young girl and said, "Good morning." Quietly she returned his greeting. Then he asked her, "What are you doing?"

As she pointed toward the sunrise, the girl said simply, "The sun is coming up and the tide is going out. If I don't pick these starfish up and throw them into the water, they'll die."

In his wisdom, the old man looked down at the girl and shook his head slowly as she reached for another starfish. "Young lady," he said, "there are thousands of starfish and just one of you. Don't you see that you can't possibly make a difference?"

Briefly, the girl looked up into his eyes, then bent over again, grabbed a starfish, and flung it into the sea. As she passed him on her way back up the beach, she stopped for just a moment. With a gentle smile she assured him, "I made a difference for *that* one."

One by one, she was throwing starfish into the sea.

At first the writer was a bit annoyed. Who did this young whippersnapper think she was talking to? But he could see she meant no disrespect. Something about her quiet determination troubled him. He walked back to his studio, deep in thought. As he played the scene over and over in his mind that day, he kept thinking about what she had said.

The best part of the story happened the next morning. As the sun began to rise, there were *two* people throwing starfish into the sea—the old man and the young girl, together.

This is a story that reveals the eighth secret of the pyramid, *initiative*. The young girl exercised an ability that is always within us: the ability to take action. It is the difference between knowing what to do and *doing what you know*. Initiative is a pivotal element in any kind of teamwork, because when you use your initiative you set off a chain reaction in others that leads to true synergy.

145

The Key to Living Heroically

When you exercise your initiative you demonstrate the courage to make decisions and take action, regardless of the odds or the immensity of the challenge before you. It is the very essence of something I call living heroically. Our children need some real heroes today. We all do! Recently I heard a very startling statistic. According to a recent study, over 90 percent of the news we hear each day from the media is negative. When you stop to think about it, how often is the front page of your newspaper filled with stories of heroism and teamwork?

It's so rare, it truly stands out. In my seminars I ask participants if they remember the story of a young family trapped by a blizzard in northern California and their bravery and heroism in surviving against the odds. The father walked more than fifty miles through the bitter cold to find help while his wife stayed behind with their children in a tiny shelter they had made of snow and ice. She pushed her rising fears aside to care for her children for almost a week before help finally came. Everyone I talked to was deeply moved by this story of incredible initiative.

What is it that makes people heroes? What do they do? Think for a moment about your heroes. Who are they? How do you feel about them? Is heroism a quality reserved only for a special few? Is it the product of some special combination of DNA—or is there choice involved? Can we somehow cultivate our ability to live heroic lives? Are there heroes around us whom we simply don't see? Is heroism a rare quality, or does it exist within each of us?

Most of us grew up thinking of famous people as our heroes. We wanted to be like these big success stories, the star athletes, movie stars, or political leaders—people of great influence, power, or wealth. As we grew older, we expanded our vision of heroism to include those who found the strength to handle terrible calamities. From the unemployed worker in Pittsburgh who ran back into a blazing inferno not once or twice, but four times to save children he had never seen before, to the Jewish prisoners at Auschwitz who selflessly offered their own meager meals to others in worse shape than they were—these stories of courage in the face of great adversity inspire us. They touch that special part of us that desperately wants to see the best in human beings—the part that wants to know that maybe, just maybe, it's in us, too.

Can we somehow cultivate our ability to live heroic lives?

Ultimately, all real heroes have one thing in common. *They become heroic when they do something with every ounce of their heart and soul that somehow makes a positive difference for someone else.* Initiative is the key to living heroically. The combination of these two simple yet unbelievably powerful elements—doing something with 100 percent of your heart and soul, and somehow making a positive difference for someone else—brings out the very best inside us. It is in these moments of initiative that we become true team players, catapulting the heroism within us to new heights.

When you exercise your initiative, it is incredibly empowering for you and those you touch. At any moment, you can choose to live heroically. You do not have to overcome terrible adversity or receive recognition from others. Instead, initiative demands only that you be fully present and that you take action unselfishly with your whole spirit. It is something you can choose to experience daily and can develop as a part of who you are. Just as you strengthen a muscle through concentrated repetition, so, too, can you build your initiative. When tough challenges arise, you will handle them with confidence and energy.

One of the most valuable ways to exercise your initiative is to acknowledge and recognize initiative in others. Through this practice, you will naturally strengthen your Pygmalion spirit and begin to spot heroism in others that they do not yet see in themselves. As you express appreciation for their genius, you will help build their self-worth. Instead of feeling taken for granted, the people around you will know they are truly important. In turn, you will discover qualities of heroism and excellence in them that you can work to develop in yourself.

The Unquenchable Spirit

The first time I began to look at heroes a little differently was in my sophomore year at Stanford University. I had volunteered to teach swimming to children at the Community Association for the Retarded in Palo Alto, California. The program was the realization of the dream of a very special woman. Her name was Betty Wright, and she had battled for more than fifteen years to gather the funding to build and operate this all-volunteer program. She was in her sixties when the state-of-the-art swimming facility was finally constructed according to her design. With her white hair and wrinkled features she looked like a delicate, almost frail grandmother. That impression lasted about five seconds. When she spoke, she radiated a fiery spirit and unstoppable energy. What a dynamo!

I met Betty when she was sixty-five. I had joined about fifteen other new volunteers for our first training session at the facility. I had been involved in aquatics my whole life, so I felt confident I knew just about everything I would need to know. I remember thinking as I waited for the training to begin that perhaps I could pick up a small tip here and there about working with disabled students. But, by and large, I felt certain nothing would surprise me. I was pretty cocky. I was also about to receive a rude awakening!

Betty walked in pushing a 16-year-old boy named Colin in his wheelchair. Colin was both blind and deaf, and his cerebral palsy was so severe that he seemed completely unable to control his body. We watched without a word as she rolled Colin right up to the edge of the pool. We expected her to turn and speak to us, but instead she tilted Colin's wheelchair and abruptly dumped him into the water! I just about dove in after him, but Betty must have caught my look of terror because she snapped, "Sit down and watch!"

As Colin hit the water he splashed around, making a loud gurgling sound that made me even more nervous. But in a moment, we could see that he wasn't in trouble at all. In fact, he was turning backward somersaults over and over in pure delight. The gurgling was the sound of unrestrained laughter! We watched in awe as this blind and deaf boy shot like a missile to the bottom of the eleven-foot-deep end and pulled up the drain cover to play with. He knew every inch of that pool as if he were guided by radar. Each second he spent in the water was a moment of complete ecstasy.

He was turning backward somersaults over and over in pure delight.

Betty let us watch Colin for several minutes before she said another word. We were mesmerized. Finally she sent one of her assistants into the water with Colin and turned to speak to us. "Don't ever think that these children can't learn!" she crackled. "This isn't water to Colin; it's paradise. People like you make this possible. You don't have to be a great swimmer or an experienced teacher to help these kids. Colin has had hundreds of volunteer swimming teachers just like you over the years. Each one was a little bit different. But every one of them had one special thing in common. *They cared*. That's what we want from you—your caring. That's what makes this program work. Nothing else matters as much. That's how you'll turn this pool into paradise."

Pursue Your Passion

Over the years, I have come to revere both Colin and Betty. Each demonstrated in unique ways the power of initiative to inspire and broaden the spectrum of possibility. They helped me to see that there is a hero in all of us whenever we choose to immerse ourselves fully in pursuing our passion.

Colin has become my "joy hero." Many of us have forgotten how to truly appreciate the little things in life. The indelible image of Colin turning those backward somersaults in complete and utter delight constantly reminds me what pure joy really is. *When we encourage celebration of simple joys and recognition of small wins, we help create an atmosphere where initiative is alive and vibrant.* It is the kind of environment people enjoy immersing themselves in each day.

Betty Wright's example is with me always as my "care hero." She exemplifies the unstoppable force of initiative based upon simple caring. She has helped me see that everyone—yes, everyone!—is a leader. Whether at home, at work, in community or volunteer projects, on the playing field, in church or synagogue, with friends— we are all leaders at certain times and in certain situations. We all have the chance to use our initiative to become the kind of leaders who ignite heroic spirit in others and ourselves.

The fuel that enables us to fully exercise our initiative is *energy*. Yet most of us have been taught that our level of energy is more a product of chance than choice. We look at energy in much the same way as we view the weather. We hope for a sunny, bright day for our family picnic just as we hope we'll somehow have the energy we need to be at our best.

Most of us have been taught that our level of energy is more a product of chance than choice.

Energy is something you can choose to cultivate and build within you consistently every day. Amidst the dizzying acceleration of information, technology, and change that is our current and future reality, energy has never been more important. It has been predicted that we will double the total amount of information that has been accumulated throughout history within the next five years. The single most powerful tool to deal positively with this kind of explosive change is our own energy and vitality.

Think of how you would feel springing to life each morning, knowing you have all the energy you need to handle whatever challenges come your way. This kind of vibrancy is possible for you through three fundamental keys to inexhaustible energy.

1. Eat for Optimum Energy

The first is adopting a diet that supports you in feeling light and energized at a cellular level. Your diet must provide the essential raw material you need to sustain energy over the long haul. By consciously eating a variety of wholesome, nutrient-rich foods you allow your body to find the natural balance and harmony that was intended for it. If you've been eating a poor diet of fatty and highly processed foods, or are feeling run-down, stressed, and fatigued, your body is already screaming out to you for cleansing.

A diet rich in fresh vegetables and fruits (especially homegrown or organically farmed), whole grains, legumes, fresh juices, pure water, and super foods loaded with natural trace minerals, amino acids, and chlorophyll is your best defense against disease and your greatest support for a strong and healthy immune system. It is fundamental to maintaining vibrant energy.

2. Move to Feel Alive

The second key for cultivating the energy to fuel initiative is movement. It has been said that people don't really grow old, they just stop moving! Think of the times in your life when you actively engaged in some form of regular exercise and physical movement. Wasn't your experience of life richer and more satisfying? Did you feel more alert and clear, mentally? When challenges arose, were you more flexible and at peace emotionally?

Anthony Robbins says, "Emotion is created by motion." He is referring to the fact that when we change our physiology we alter our biochemistry. Suddenly sixty trillion cells are flooded with new information and fresh stimulation. This is why movement is the single fastest way to change your emotional state and revitalize your initiative. All of us have had days when we felt so exhausted we didn't think we could move off the sofa. We couldn't even muster the energy to reach out for the remote control—we're talking major russet couch potato, here! But, have you ever been in that kind of near-comatose state when something suddenly startled you? Perhaps your child screamed or there was an unexpected knock at the door. *Boom!*— you sprang into action with a level of energy you had thought impossible only moments before.

Movement and exercise also stimulate creativity and solution orientation. They can recharge your initiative when you feel stifled or blocked. For the past twelve years I have been a dedicated runner. Each time I head out for a run I feel my spirit soar as I relax into a state where I let go of trying to force answers and instead allow a quiet natural integration to take place. Ideas and concerns that had been swirling about helter-skelter within me seem to settle into a workable order. Inevitably when I return I am rejuvenated and inspired. If I've been stuck on a problem, suddenly I am back in motion, seeing new possibilities and ignited with fresh initiative.

3. Develop a Compelling "Why"

The third fundamental key to activating your energy is defining and developing a truly compelling "why"—a deeply inspiring purpose for your life. In his book *The On-Purpose Person,* Kevin W. McCarthy begins the final chapter with a wonderful quote from Norman Vincent Peale that captures the heart of living with a compelling why.

> We are here to be excited from youth to old age, to have an insatiable curiosity about the world. . . . We are also here to help others by practicing a friendly attitude. And every person is born for a purpose. Everyone has a God-given potential, in essence, built into them. And if we are to live life to its fullest, we must realize that potential.

Your personal compelling why is the most pivotal of the three keys to building extraordinary initiative. Without it you will likely fall into the black hole of procrastination and indecision. Gradually you may feel your sense of self-worth shrivel as you become resigned to merely existing rather than truly living. With a compelling why you will overcome obstacles you thought insurmountable and break through the fear and doubt that pose the greatest threat to fully exercising your initiative.

Several years ago my wife and I decided to participate in a ropes adventure course taught by two phenomenal teachers, Drs. Bill Baker and Terry Henderson. In the one-day class, Carole and I were challenged with all sorts of fascinating games to stretch our creativity, build team synergy, and expose the often unnecessary internal rules and restrictions we place on ourselves. The morning session consisted solely of "ground elements," activities that kept us safely in contact with Mother Earth. After lunch, however, we were told that we would move to the "high elements" such as climbing telephone poles and balancing with a partner while inching along a thin cable thirty feet above the ground. In the final element, called the pamper pole, we would scale a fifty-foot pole about ten inches in diameter. When we reached the top our goal was to somehow find the courage (and coordination!) to lift ourselves up and stand atop the swaying timber. Then when we became centered, we were to hurl ourselves out into space, desperately trying to grab a trapeze that hung tantalizingly twelve feet directly in front of us.

During these high elements you wear a harness, and safety is utmost in the minds of the instructors. But when you are up there all alone staring at that trapeze, the harness doesn't feel especially comforting!

At lunch, Carole and I talked about how much we had enjoyed the morning session. But she made it emphatically clear she had no intention of participating in any of the high elements. For as long as she could remember she had been petrified of heights. She would happily support everyone in any way she could, but she was not climbing any telephone poles! Carole is also a person who is not about to be forced or coerced through peer pressure. I was quite certain her active participation was done for the day.

The first high element that was planned for us that afternoon was a relatively simple experience wherein we were to climb a thirty-foot telephone pole, then walk across another telephone pole suspended horizontally and attached to another upright pole. The apparatus looked like oversized football goalposts. One by one, we made our way to the top and wobbled across while our teammates cheered and encouraged our every step. After we made it to the other side we were invited to make our way back to the middle of the horizontal pole and to fall forward toward the ground in a swan dive position. After a moment of free flight, the instructors would ease us back to earth, setting us down gently to the applause and delight of our teammates.

For as long as she could remember she had been petrified of heights.

When it came time for Carole's turn she just smiled and politely declined. I figured that was the end of that, when suddenly she astonished me by changing her mind and stepping forward to the pole. As she reached up for a handhold she announced that she was going to climb up two or three steps, period. Everyone rallied around her, offering great support. To my complete amazement she ever so slowly edged a good eight feet up the pole. There she stopped, frozen solid as she clutched the pole in a death grip. It was clear she wasn't going any higher, but she wasn't in any hurry to come down, either. No manner of encouragement could make her budge.

Just then, our daughter Kelsey walked into the ropes course area with the baby-sitter we had hired for the day. It turned out that the sitter had a family emergency and had to bring Kelsey to us.

Instantly Carole spotted Kelsey. I saw their eyes meet as Kelsey looked up in wonder and confusion at her mother gripping that telephone pole. As she listened to everyone cheering, she smiled up at Carole, beaming at her mother with love and pride.

I still am stunned by what happened next. Carole let out a deep breath and began to climb, up, up, and up. She didn't stop until she stood at the very top, thirty feet above the ground. I don't know whose heart was pounding harder, Carole's or mine! The team was going absolutely nuts now, roaring their approval and excitement. I never in my wildest dreams thought I would see anything like this.

Carole let out a deep breath

and began to climb,

up, up, and up.

At this point I thought her victory was complete and she would carefully make her way back down the pole. I knew there was no way she would actually attempt to walk across. But then, Kelsey's little voice called out, "You can do it, Mommy!" The next thing I knew, Carole tiptoed around the vertical pole, holding it tightly behind her back. All at once she let go and started to inch forward, teetering and swaying with each tiny step. Slowly, slowly she moved farther out along the pole until she stood in the very center looking down at all of us. Finally, with a wild scream, she leaned out and jumped off. The instructor eased her down amid total bedlam. Everyone rushed to her, hugging her in joy and congratulations. I broke into tears as Kelsey leaped into her mother's arms. It is a moment I will treasure as long as I live.

Later that day I asked Carole what in the world caused her to go up that pole. She replied, "When I looked down at Kelsey, as terrified as I was, I knew that I could not bear to teach her my fears. And so I climbed. Somehow I felt that if I broke through, she would, too."

There are few forces on earth as powerful as a truly compelling why. Discover yours and you will immediately free yourself to live a life of purpose and joy fueled by the never-ending energy needed to support your initiative.

11

Secret #9:

Intentness

When you look at Coach Wooden's unparalleled achievements—ten National Championships, the only individual to be elected to the NCAA Basketball Hall of Fame as both a player and a coach, sixteen Conference Championships— it is easy to assume that his path to greatness was a smooth one, with few serious obstacles to overcome. In reality, his life is a powerful testimony to the importance of *intentness* in achieving true excellence. It took Coach Wooden thirty years to win his first National Championship. He did not become a legend overnight.

Like all great leaders, he overcame countless difficulties and persevered through many setbacks before the successes began to snowball.

In 1960 he entered his twenty-seventh year of coaching. Through eleven years at the high school level, two years at Indiana State University, and thirteen years at UCLA, his teams had compiled an excellent won-lost percentage and earned several conference titles. At UCLA, he had coached his team into the NCAA tournament on a number of occasions. Yet they had never won The Big One. In fact, his 1959 team had just completed the poorest season in his UCLA career, winning fourteen games and losing twelve.

Press and alumni alike began to question whether Coach Wooden had what it took to build a program into the dominating national powerhouse they wanted. Following the disappointing 1959 season, he decided to analyze every detail of his program and coaching methodology. Driven by his belief that "Failure is not fatal, but failure to change might be," he dug into his notebooks and records, searching for any clues or patterns that could help him understand where to make adjustments. After months of study he concluded that despite the subpar year, he was on the right track and needed only to make a few small changes in his practice drills to give his players more rest as the season progressed.

At first his efforts appeared to pay off. Over the next two seasons his teams showed great improvement. In 1960–61, UCLA finished with a record of eighteen wins and eight losses, narrowly missing the Conference Championship. In the 1961–62 season, the team made it all the way to the semifinals of the NCAA Tournament, losing to eventual champion Cincinnati by two points. Perhaps now his critics would be satisfied. After twenty-eight years in coaching, Wooden had brought his team within one game of the NCAA title. Hopes were high that 1962–63 would be the breakthrough year.

"Failure is not fatal, but failure to change might be."

It was not to be. Just when he appeared ready to ascend the final step, he was pushed back once more. Though UCLA enjoyed a fine season, winning twenty and losing nine, they were eliminated in the first round of the NCAAs. Once again, rumblings were heard around Los Angeles that Wooden just didn't have the ability to win a national title.

In our culture, pressure from the outside becomes the most intense for teams and individuals who approach the top without going all the way. Fans and press seem to have less patience for near champions than for second division teams. The Buffalo Bills, Denver Broncos, and Minnesota Vikings reached the Super Bowl twelve times collectively over the past twenty-five years. Yet they are most often thought of as "losers" because they've never won the crown. Prior to the amazing final twelve years of his career, John Wooden was seen by many in the same light.

When his 1963–64 starting team was announced, the rumblings grew even louder. UCLA had no starter over 6'5" tall! No NCAA championship team in the modern era had ever been so small. Because of their speed, they were picked to be a strong team, but definitely not a champion.

Fans and press seem to have less patience for near champions than for second division teams.

Thirty games later UCLA had beaten back every challenger and silenced every doubter. They were the undefeated National Champions. In his thirtieth year as a coach, John Wooden had finally proved he could, indeed, win The Big One.

Over the next eleven years his UCLA teams would go on to compile the most amazing run of championship performances in NCAA history. Wooden would be hailed as "the Wizard of Westwood," widely recognized as the greatest basketball coach ever.

Be True to Your Convictions

Abraham Lincoln once said, "Almost everyone can handle adversity. But, to test a person's true character, give him power." During the triumphant final twelve years of his career, Coach Wooden remained as flexible in approach and immovable in his intent as he had been in the first thirty. Through it all, the adversity and the glory, he remained committed to gaining peace of mind from the internal knowledge that he had given his all to become the best of which he was capable. It was this intentness that allowed Wooden to feel successful regardless of whether UCLA won the championship or fell short. He was every bit as proud of his 1961–62 team, which lost in the semifinals by two points, as he was of any of his championship teams. While others would judge his success strictly by his NCAA titles, he knew that ultimate success was something he would feel in his own heart by giving his maximum effort to live according to his true intent. He held firmly to the same fundamental intent for each of his players and his teams. This was more important to him than undefeated seasons or championship banners. He believed those would come naturally if he remained true to his convictions. Victories and defeats were temporary to Coach Wooden; his intentness was permanent.

Like Jackie Robinson, Coach Wooden constantly exercised his determination to resist temptation and to stay on his course. During the years he coached Kareem Abdul-Jabbar (née Lew Alcindor), UCLA won an astonishing eighty-eight games while losing only two. The first of those losses came during the middle of Jabbar's junior year when the Bruins met the University of Houston Cougars in one of the most celebrated events in college basketball history. The game was highly promoted because it was the first to be held in a giant indoor baseball stadium, the Houston Astrodome. More than 52,000 fans jammed into the arena that day to watch the nation's number one and number two teams battle it out. Jabbar played despite a badly scratched retina that had kept him out of practice for more than a week before the game. Even though his timing and endurance were obviously affected, the contest was not decided until the final seconds when the great Cougar star Elvin Hayes hit a pressure-packed shot to give Houston the victory by two points.

Coach Wooden was gracious in defeat, choosing to give Houston full credit rather than making excuses. For the rest of the season, Houston was ranked number one and became the solid favorite to win the NCAA title. Basketball insiders were convinced that UCLA would have to change its approach if it hoped to control Elvin Hayes and upset the Cougars in the NCAA Tournament. Wooden remained intent, focusing not on beating Houston, but on assisting his team to become the best of which they were capable. He stuck determinedly to his own game. He believed that diligent preparation and repetition of fundamentals were far more important than fancy game plans. Despite the loss at the Astrodome and growing pressure from the press and alumni, Coach Wooden felt UCLA would prevail by playing its own style with improved execution. When the Bruins met Houston once again that season in the semifinals of the NCAA Tournament, they won by thirty-two points! Buoyed by Wooden's calm assurance, his players were able to learn from their earlier defeat and emerge with greater confidence than ever before. His patient and irrepressible intentness enabled them to draw new strength from adversity.

Life's Greatest Blessings

Several years ago I heard a beautiful expression of this principle when I attended a church service in Anchorage, Alaska, just before Thanksgiving. The minister shared many thoughts about the true meaning of the holiday that really struck home that day. She said that most of us had been raised to look at Thanksgiving as a time to give thanks for the special people in our lives, for our good fortune, and for all the blessings we have received.

"Indeed," she went on, "it is important to appreciate all the wonderful gifts we have been given. *But, this Thanksgiving, I suddenly realized that perhaps we should give our greatest thanks for all the obstacles and setbacks we have faced along life's path, for it is from these that we have grown the most.*"

In my seminars, I tell participants about that Thanksgiving thought—genuinely giving thanks for life's toughest obstacles—because this is such a beautiful expression of a fundamental truth about great leadership. *When adversity strikes, the quality and intensity of our true intent ultimately plays a far greater role than does talent or ability in determining how effectively we impact others.* Napoleon Hill once wrote, "With every adversity is planted the seed of an equivalent or greater benefit." It is our intentness that nourishes this seed, increasing our ability to gain strength from adversity.

Turn Setbacks to Your Advantage

In his autobiography, *Kareem,* Jabbar described how Coach Wooden's patient and unshakable intentness affected him when the College Basketball Rules Committee banned the dunk shot just before his junior season at UCLA. It was widely believed that the rule change was primarily instituted to lessen Jabbar's dominance on the court. Wooden immediately saw the rule change as an opportunity for Jabbar to rise to a higher level. Kareem wrote, "At the time, Coach Wooden told me it would only make me a better player, helping me develop an even softer touch around the basket. This I could use to good advantage in the pros, where I could also, once again, use the dunk shot. He was right. It didn't hurt me. I worked twice as hard on banking my shots off the glass, on turnaround jump shots, and on my hook. It made me a better all-around player."

In business, your determination and intentness will be frequently challenged by factors outside your control. Just as the "no dunk" rule pushed Kareem Abdul-Jabbar to develop more of his skills and abilities, short-term economic downturns, revolutionary new technology, and constantly changing political environments will test the limits of your persistence and resolve. It is your underlying intent that enables you to pursue your goals and objectives through these inevitable challenges without abandoning your deepest principles. Living with genuine intentness demands that you be true to your own word. It is the secret to replacing procrastination with passion. When your intent is strong enough, what you say to yourself, you will do.

How, then, do you solidify your intent in the face of great adversity? How do you continue to pursue your goals with vitality and determination even when losses are mounting and prospects for success seem discouragingly dim? As a leader, how do you direct your team's focus toward its true intent rather than succumbing to the obstacles that seem so oppressive and consuming?

Build Unstoppable Momentum

Once again, the answer is found in questions, as I learned during the two years I worked with Anthony Robbins. One of the great gifts I received from him was a new awareness of the impact the questions we ask have upon our lives. Robbins has said, "The quality of my life is determined by the quality of the questions I consistently ask myself." This principle is every bit as true when it is applied to teams. In my own seminars I help participants discover that the quality of our *teams* is determined by the questions we consistently ask one another. As leaders, we must continually ask questions that enable rather than restrict. When inevitable moments of hardship arise for our organization and ourselves, we can use the power of questions to draw out a special quality from within to transform doubt into determination, fear into fortitude. That special quality is *resiliency*. Resiliency builds inspiration and toughness. It is that unstoppable ability we all possess to keep on coming back. *Resiliency is derived from our intent.*

The single greatest challenge to our resiliency and ultimately to our intentness is our own doubt. Unchecked, doubt can breed hopelessness, which can cause us to give up on our goals and dreams. When this occurs, we become detached, pessimistic, and sarcastic. This is a downward spiral that is repeated every day in the business community, in relationships, and within ourselves.

A simple set of questions can help reverse this spiral and bring us into alignment with our true intent. I call these the "Winner's Mind-Set Questions."

Break the Downward Spiral of HIQs and HAQs

1. **"Will this work?" HIQ—Hopelessness-Inducing Question (when said with doubt, fear, and skepticism)**

2. **"Will this ever work?" HAQ—Hopelessness Assured Question**

3. **"How will I make this work?" PÍQ—Possibility-Inducing Question**

4. **"How will I contribute so that we make this work for the team and our customers?" EPIQ—Exciting Possibility-Inducing Question**

Would you rather surround yourself with HIQs and HAQs or take charge and create a life of PÍQs or, better yet, EPIQs?

As a leader, it is essential that you listen for questions 1 and 2 from your team. They are important signs that doubt is brewing and that intentness is being shaken by organizational uncertainty. Question 1, Will this work?, is a HIQ (pronounced "hick"), a Hopelessness-Inducing Question.

If the words are spoken with genuine curiosity, it is simply an innocent question. As with any communication, *what* is said is far less important than *how* it is said. When the question is asked consistently with doubt, fear, or skepticism, the seed of hopelessness has been planted. The underlying meaning has been transformed from an open, unbiased question to a doubt-filled presupposition: This probably *won't* work, will it? The question has become a HIQ. It festers and inflames with constant repetition.

Gradually, the seed of hopelessness takes root. The Reverend Robert Schuller has noted that human beings have a magnificent capacity to add superlatives to our observations, questions, and evaluations. When the basic HIQ—Will this work?—is asked repeatedly with growing doubt and pessimism brewing below the surface, the second question begins to replace it. The addition of one word—*ever*—makes a profound difference in the depth of personal and organizational hopelessness. The new question is, Will this *ever* work? We call this question a HAQ (pronounced "hack")—a Hopelessness Assured Question! At this point, the question has become a statement of learned helplessness. Though the words "Will this ever work?" are uttered, the real meaning has become, This will *never* work.

When HAQs are voiced consistently throughout an organization, synergy and momentum come to a grinding halt. Employees put in their time, but give only the bare minimum. This is an organization in trouble. HIQs and

HAQs are running rampant, sapping personal accountability and the vitality that accompanies a sense of positive expectation. The team desperately needs leadership to reestablish its true intent and to reignite initiative.

The Winner's Mind-Set Questions: PÍQs and EPIQs

The transformation begins with an injection of personal responsibility through the introduction of the PÍQ (pronounced "peak")—How will I make this work?—a Possibility-Inducing Question. With this simple change, you shake yourself free from feelings of lethargy and hopelessness. Suddenly you are back in the game, using your resourcefulness and energy to tackle the toughest challenges instead of sitting on the bench. The PÍQ enables you to rediscover your initiative. When HIQs and HAQs are replaced by PÍQs in your organization, a significant emotional shift occurs that creates momentum and generates results. It is an important step, but even more is possible.

In chapter 16, we will learn about the almost magical transformation that takes place within us when we adopt principles of competitive greatness into our hearts. These principles combine to create a new model of teamwork and leadership which I call the *relay paradigm.* Fueled by absolute certainty that we will come through for the team, and inspired by a vision that extends beyond ourselves to others, we free ourselves to draw almost unlimited energy from competition and challenge. When we learn to habitually ask ourselves the fourth and final Winner's Mind-Set Question, we automatically ignite the Relay Paradigm within us. We cue ourselves to reassociate with our true intent.

PÍQs get us started by firing up our initiative. But the effects of PÍQs tend to be short-lived. When we bring our teammates and our dedication to serve them into our awareness by asking, How will I contribute so that *we* make this work for the *team* and our *customers?* we have created an EPIQ (pronounced "epic")—an Exciting Possibility-Inducing Question. Like such great epic films as *Schindler's List, Gone with the Wind, Gandhi,* or *Dances with Wolves,* EPIQs last. These classics have both action and heart. As EPIQs become more of a habit, initiative and intent combine to enable you to create your own masterpiece.

Strengthen Organizational Intent with Legendary Leadership

In his remarkable book *Leadership Is an Art,* Max DePree tells the story of the great furniture manufacturing company, Herman Miller, of which he has been a part for more than forty years. This is an organization that exemplifies the EPIQ spirit. Herman Miller is widely recognized as one of the best places in the United States to work. The company has received many awards for extraordinary quality and has had the seventh highest total return to investors of all Fortune 500 companies in the past decade.

At the heart of Herman Miller's exceptional success is an organizational intentness that demonstrates legendary leadership principles. Just as the scoreboard was less important to Coach Wooden than assisting his players and staff to become the best of which they were capable, at Herman Miller, products and profits are less important than people. The most striking characteristic of Herman Miller is the effort and dedication of its leadership to serve its employees, and through them, their customers. The company's management reinforces three key principles, constantly creating special awareness of the organization's fundamental intent.

- Relationships count far more than structure. (In other words, people are more important than position.)

- Effectiveness comes through empowering others.

- Productivity is important; giving space to giants is essential. (This means that allowing people the time and freedom to develop their talents is more important than short-term pushes for increased productivity.)

Few companies work as diligently and consistently at providing such clarity of intent to their employees. But, at Herman Miller, leadership's constant reinforcement of organizational intent inspires employees to stretch, grow, and contribute. As a result, every member of the Herman Miller team feels a heightened sense of responsibility to serve others.

DePree describes their philosophy this way:

- Being faithful is more important than being successful. If we are successful in the world's eyes but unfaithful in terms of what we believe, then we fail in our efforts at insidership (truly building a team).

- Corporations can and should have a redemptive purpose. We need to weigh the pragmatic in the clarifying light of the moral. We must understand that reaching our potential is more important than reaching our goals.

- We need to become vulnerable to each other. We owe each other the chance to reach our potential.

- Belonging requires us to be willing and ready to risk. Risk is like change; it's not a choice.

- Belonging requires intimacy. Being an insider is not a spectator sport. It means adding value. It means being fully and personally accountable. It means forgoing superficiality.

- Last, we need to be learners together. The steady process of becoming goes on in most of us throughout our lifetime. We need to be searching for maturity, openness, and sensitivity.

Bound together by this empowering intent, the company continues to excel through good and bad economic times. It is a genuine example of EPIQ success.

Indefatigable intentness is derived from defining a purpose or mission that is deeply compelling. This gives your goals both direction and inspiration. When leaders conduct themselves in harmony with the true intent of their personal mission, their impact on others is dramatically increased. They demonstrate almost endless initiative, fueled by their ever-present intent. This, more than any other single factor, contributed to Coach Wooden's unique success. His players knew, without question, that their efforts to become the best of which they were capable were more important to Wooden than winning any game, award, or championship. As a result, each knew that they, themselves—not circumstance—determined their success and their importance to the team. He was intent on helping them reach their potential, and he used goals as achievable steps leading to that higher mission.

The Cell Tech Success Story

One of the great privileges I have had in my business career has been to work with two individuals who epitomize the same kind of intentness and initiative in their field as Coach Wooden brought to college basketball. Daryl and Marta Kollman are the co-founders of Cell Tech, which has become the United States' largest producer of an unusual, high-energy food: blue-green algae. Their story is one of inexhaustible intentness in the face of immense challenges.

After earning his master's degree in science from Harvard University, Daryl decided that the greatest gift he could offer to others would be to become a teacher. Teaching was the perfect fusion of his love for children and his passion for learning. As he immersed himself in teaching, he became deeply concerned that his students' ability to remain focused in the classroom appeared to be diminishing. He had tremendous faith in the potential of young people to learn, but he knew that something was chipping away at their attention span and power of concentration.

At Harvard, his principal areas of study had been biochemistry and nutrition. In his research on the "green revolution," he had discovered that although the widespread use of nitrogen-based chemical fertilizers had radically increased the quantity of food produced per acre, it had just as dramatically affected food quality, by robbing fruits and vegetables of much of their natural nutritive value. As his concern about the decreasing attentiveness of students deepened, he became convinced that diminishing nutrition was a central cause.

Finally, encouraged with unconditional support from Marta, he made the decision to leave teaching and devote himself to improving the quality of nutrition worldwide. In this way, he could attack on a major scale a primary cause, rather than swatting at the symptoms of educational sluggishness. During the past twenty years the Kollmans have pursued this purpose with indomitable intentness.

The Kollmans' search for a source of nutrition unaffected by the use of chemical fertilizers and pesticides led them to the study of algae. For years, their young family lived in virtual isolation in the desert in New Mexico as they conducted extensive research on algae as a high-energy food source. Living in a little trailer in the midst of dust and extreme heat, the dream of making a profound difference in the quality of life for humankind must have seemed all but unreachable. Yet their resolve remained unshakable.

In 1976 the Kollmans were introduced to a natural strain of blue-green algae that contained more nutritive value than any food they had ever seen. It was a completely unique strain that grew in massive quantities in only one place on earth, Upper Klamath Lake in southern Oregon.

This Super Blue Green™ Algae had an immediate and profound effect on both Daryl and Marta's overall health and vitality. They moved their family to Klamath Falls and over the past fifteen years have built a company that now harvests several million pounds of algae each year, supplying over 100,000 Cell Tech distributors throughout North America.

Cultivating the Winning Ingredient

Every step of the way, the Kollmans were besieged with opposition and adversity. Without their extraordinary intentness, they would have given up long before Cell Tech became a successful company. Though in many parts of the world, algae had long been a food staple, in the United States it was largely unknown as a source of nutrition and energy. Before Cell Tech built its vast network of distributors, most Americans thought algae was something you scrubbed off shower tiles or tried to keep from growing in your swimming pool. The task of reeducating a culture with very strong eating habits and conditioning is immense. Even in their own southern Oregon community they were initially looked on with uneasiness and suspicion. But, like the young starfish thrower in the previous chapter, the Kollmans remained intent on making a difference, one step at a time.

During the early years, they handled every facet of the business completely on their own—harvesting the algae from the lake; fighting for the rights to secure harvest sites; building intricate harvest equipment from spare parts; developing a unique freeze-drying process to keep the algae's nutritive value pure; filling hundreds of thousands of capsules with the algae by hand; marketing, selling, and accounting for the results of their efforts.

At one point they were so low on cash, they felt they had no choice but to sell the business to investors. The new owners saw that the Kollmans' knowledge and expertise was critical to maintaining the confidence of the distributors following the sale, so they kept them aboard as the company's operating officers. Daryl's impassioned vision was the flame that kept the spirit of the organization burning through good times and bad. Marta's unmatched knowledge of Cell Tech administrative operations and her extraordinary attention to detail deepened distributors' trust in the integrity of the company. They were a perfectly balanced team. The Kollmans continued to run Cell Tech as employees for several years, saving every penny they could to somehow gather the capital to buy the company back.

Gradually the new owners sought to exercise greater control over day-to-day operations. With their focus mainly on short-term profits, they saw extensive product development and training as unnecessary expenses. A rift began to develop over the direction and ultimate intent of the company. When they cut off all funding for research, the Kollmans decided they could go no further. For nine excruciating months they battled through tortuous negotiations. It was an incredibly difficult time, but they refused to give up on their dream. Their intent was too strong. Eight long years after being forced to relinquish ownership, they bought the company back. Together, they have led Cell Tech to outstanding growth ever since.

A gentle and shy man by nature, Daryl developed himself into an outstanding speaker so that he could share his algae story with people all over the world. Educated as a scientist and a teacher, he never conceived of himself as a businessman or marketer. Yet today he and Marta lead a company that is a striking success story in a part of the country devastated by economic recession. Their company is now making a global difference. Cell Tech supplies an impoverished village of three thousand in Nicaragua with enough Super Blue Green Algae for every man, woman, and child, every day. The new source of nutrition has had a striking impact on general health in the village. What's more, in the village schools, the children's test scores in reading and mathematics have risen an average of better than 15 percent since they began eating the algae. The Kollmans' dream is becoming a reality.

Leadership is the art of risking failure to live according to your true values and intent. Unwavering intent gives you the strength to overcome your greatest fears or weaknesses. It is an absolutely essential secret of a winning life.

12

Secret #10:

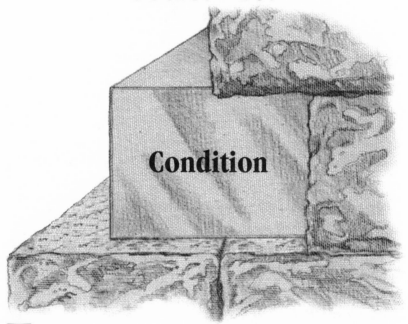

Condition

Let's play a little game together that will introduce you to the tenth secret of a winning life, *condition*. Read the following sentence through *one time* quickly.

> FINISHED FILES ARE THE RESULT
> OF YEARS OF SCIENTIFIC STUDY
> COMBINED WITH THE EXPERIENCE
> OF MANY YEARS OF EXPERTS

It's a simple, almost silly little sentence of no earthshaking importance. Now that you've read it through once with no specific outcome, let's try something a little different. Read the sentence once more, straight through, but as you read this time, count the times you see the letter F. Before you read any further, go ahead and do that now.

How many Fs did you count—two Fs? three Fs? four, five, or six Fs? How about seven? Whatever number of Fs you counted, let's do one more thing just to double-check. As you read the sentence again one last time, first count the times you see the word *of*, and then count the total number of Fs you see.

If you are like most people in my seminars, you saw only two or three Fs when you first counted. When I asked you to double-check by first looking for the *ofs*, it was probably quite a surprise! I always enjoy the spontaneous reaction of participants when they discover all seven Fs. From every corner of the room I hear little bursts of laughter and exclamations like, "Oh, my gosh!" "I can't believe it!"

Once everyone has absorbed the surprise, I ask a simple question. "Why didn't we see all the Fs? How can we miss them when they are right there in front of us?" The answer has very little to do with our ability to read, and a great deal to do with the importance of *conditioning*. The F in the word *of* is in a mental blind spot. It is virtually invisible until we look at it in an entirely different way. Such blind spots result from very simple conditioning. When we were young, we learned to read phonetically, by sounding words out. Thus, we learned the word *of* as *ov*. We repeated the sound over and over until we had it down pat. Now, many years later, we still see the word *of* as *ov* because of the way we were conditioned.

Avoid the Trap of Familiarity

Even people who have played the game before are often surprised. Usually, the sentence appears without the last two words, and contains only six Fs. *Of experts* has been added to help people recognize how they can fall into the trap of depending on their memory instead of being present and alert. I remember being shocked when someone first used the seven-F sentence on me. I was certain I knew the game. As soon as I saw the card, I smiled to myself smugly. I thought, I'm really going to have fun watching all these people find only two or three Fs. (Of course, I too had seen only three the first time I counted!) Boy, are they going to be surprised when they find out there are really six!

When the instructor asked how many people counted two Fs, then three Fs, most of the hands went up. When he asked if anybody had found six Fs, I raised my hand in triumph along with one or two others who had seen the game before. Then he asked if anyone had counted *seven* Fs. One man way in the back raised his hand. I started to laugh, thinking, This guy is making up Fs!

In the dictionary, *conditioned* is defined as "characterized by a consistent pattern of behavior." Even though I knew the secret of the word *of* in the game, I had fallen into another consistent pattern of behavior— relying on my memory instead of using my alertness and understanding. This is a common trap for leaders. Patterns that worked yesterday may be totally inappropriate today. The last laugh was on me as I learned another lesson about the importance of conditioning.

This fun little game takes on new significance when we apply its lessons to far more important things than counting Fs. If the way we were conditioned way back when we learned to read can cause us to miss something as obvious as the F in the word *of* today, what else might we be missing? Perhaps there are opportunities and solutions constantly available to us that we simply do not yet see because of other old conditioning!

It is exciting to realize that the process of revealing the mental blind spot and discovering the answer is simply a matter of new conditioning. As soon as I asked you to look for the word *of,* the Fs practically jumped off the page. It was like adjusting the focus on your camera, suddenly bringing a blurred image into crystal clarity. Remember when I asked little red-haired Allison to pretend that she was just diving in to do her warm-up sprint as she hit the 75-meter mark in her Junior Olympic race? After years of conditioning her to focus on "not dying" at the end of each race, this new conditioning created an entirely new result. The same is possible for you in your relationships, your business, and in every aspect of your life.

Install New Conditioning

One of the major goals of this book is to introduce possibilities for new conditioning in the way you perceive leadership and success. Many of us have been conditioned to view success as something that can only be measured on the scoreboard or financial statement. With this conditioned mind-set, success means finishing first, earning the maximum profit, or outperforming your opponents. This also means that for you to win, everyone else must lose. However, for legendary leaders, success is an *inner* feeling of peace that comes from knowing you've given your best effort. It is possible for every person you work with in every moment.

Leadership is the process of installing new conditioning that enables everyone to discover and use more of their true potential. When you operate from the Wooden view of success, the direction, style, and focus of your leadership will differ sharply from the "winning is everything" concept. You will create entirely new conditioning within your organization. It is very exciting to realize that in John Wooden we have an irrefutable example of the effectiveness of this leadership paradigm. Kareem Abdul-Jabbar expressed this empowering realization beautifully when he wrote:

> It is a rare experience to meet an individual who affirms the positive values you were introduced to in childhood, as I was by the nuns at school and by my father, who was a cop. You wonder if such values work, and then you encounter an individual like John Wooden and see the success he's had as a person, not just in terms of wins and losses, but as a man trying to live his life with some balance and honor, and then you know it's possible. He was the real thing. His example in my life continues to be bright and shining.

The Importance of Balance

One of the differentiating features of Coach Wooden's leadership style is his emphasis on *balanced* conditioning. When most people think of his great UCLA teams, they think of superb athletes achieving a remarkable level of *physical* conditioning. But Coach Wooden would be the first to tell you that no amount of physical conditioning will serve you in the long run unless you are also mentally, morally, and emotionally conditioned. Conditioning is truly effective only when it is balanced.

Coach Wooden's deep-rooted belief in the importance of balanced conditioning was something he not only voiced, but put into practice through action. He once related to me a recruiting experience that demonstrates the high standards of emotional and moral conditioning he emphasized throughout his career.

During his twenty-seven years at UCLA, Coach Wooden made fewer than two dozen out-of-state recruiting trips. He disliked extra travel and having to spend time away from his family during the off-season. Whenever he did make the decision to travel to meet with a prospect, it was usually because the player was so highly prized by other universities that a visit from the head coach seemed essential. Even in these cases, Coach Wooden always viewed his primary purpose to be evaluation of the athlete's character, rather than recruitment of the player. If the prospect demonstrated solid mental, moral, and emotional condition, only then would he be offered a scholarship to UCLA.

On one such trip, Coach Wooden traveled across the country to visit a player who was widely considered the nation's top prospect in his position. The player possessed such extraordinary physical skills that most coaches believed he was a true "phenom," a can't-miss recruit—the kind of athlete around which you could build an entire program. His grades and test scores were acceptable as well, so he appeared to have the ability to succeed academically. This was absolutely essential to Coach Wooden. When the young man announced that he considered UCLA one of his top three choices, Wooden decided to make the cross-country journey.

When Coach Wooden arrived at the prospect's home, he was greeted at the door by the boy and his mother. As they walked into the living room, the mother began to ask the coach about his trip and about UCLA. Almost immediately the boy cut her off tersely, ordering her into the kitchen to fetch refreshments. That was enough for Coach Wooden. Within five minutes he was out the door, headed back to Los Angeles. He politely told this future superstar, "I have very strong feelings about the respect young men show their parents. I don't believe UCLA is the place for you. I wish you well at another university." Despite the youth's tremendous physical ability and solid academic skills, he lacked the moral and emotional conditioning the coach looked for in his recruits.

Balance Mental, Physical, Emotional, and Moral Conditioning

Recognizing the importance of balanced conditioning is every bit as crucial in the business environment as it is on the basketball floor. Yet, in the same way that many coaches make the mistake of considering only the physical conditioning of the athletes they train, many business leaders often focus solely on *mental* conditioning, failing to understand how important physical condition is in the workplace. In the past twenty to thirty years the work of such brilliant leaders as Dr. Norman Cousins, Dr. Deepak Chopra, and Dr. Bernie Siegel has created new awareness that the health and vitality of our minds play a tremendous role in our physical health. It is now becoming more and more clear that the reverse is equally important. The way we use our bodies—our physical condition—has a tremendous amount to do with the health and vitality of our minds!

In my seminars, I incorporate a great deal of physical activity. Through a variety of exercises, participants discover how much more resourceful they become when they raise the level of their physical energy. Creativity, flexibility, and mental alertness soar as we learn to cultivate improved levels of physical condition. At the same time, the enhanced physical condition directly elevates enthusiasm and teamwork. Over time, by encouraging consistent moderate exercise, healthy eating habits, and reasonable workdays which leave time for relaxation and recreation, companies do much more than lower health care costs. They bolster the resourcefulness and effectiveness of their staff. At the same time they develop greater loyalty, trust, and appreciation among employees by demonstrating their genuine concern for them as human beings. Everyone wins when holistic conditioning is an important consideration.

By the same token, no amount of physical and mental conditioning will make up for insufficient moral or emotional condition. Some of this nation's top financial strategists are in prison for their roles in the savings and loan scandals that rocked our economy. These individuals possessed exceptional knowledge about their field. They were mentally well conditioned, but lacked the moral and emotional conditioning to disdain temptation for short-term gain.

Fit the Conditioning to the Task

To develop your effectiveness as a leader, it is essential that you recognize that different roles and tasks demand different kinds of conditioning. I will always remember watching the great boxer Joe Frazier attempt to swim in a Superstars competition several years ago. Here was a magnificently conditioned athlete—capable of boxing fifteen incredibly grueling rounds with Muhammad Ali—practically drowning on national television as he tried to swim fifty yards! His conditioning simply did not fit the task he was attempting.

As a leader, you are a *conditioning coach*. By being alert to each team member's part in the overall effort, you can design a conditioning program that helps bring out his or her very best. Just as on a basketball team a quality coach develops different players to fill different roles, you can assist your business teammates to adopt conditioning that enables them to maximize their unique contributions while strengthening the team as a whole.

By viewing part of your leadership role as being a conditioning coach, you automatically enhance your long-term perspective. You become less task-oriented and more human development-oriented. As your employees tackle major projects, you recognize that their tasks are essential steps in the growth and development of their ultimate potential. You strive for top performance from yourself and the team. Yet, you place even greater value on what each member learns in the process. As a result, you emerge from each effort with sharper clarity about what fundamentals, skills, and principles are most critical to develop if you are to continue to grow. This is a critical distinction of great leadership.

> **By being alert to each team member's part in the overall effort, you can design a conditioning program that helps bring out his or her very best.**

Anthony Robbins succinctly stated a principle expressed by many human-potential leaders when he said, "Our lives are nothing but a mirror of our consistent thoughts." We have tremendous ability to condition ourselves through repetition and focus. This is especially important when we seek to develop leadership abilities. The 15 Secrets, from industriousness and enthusiasm to self-control and intentness, become truly valuable only when we condition them into our being. As we use our initiative to condition new patterns of behavior consistent with these secrets, we will gain the peace of mind and self-satisfaction that come when we know we've given the best of which we are capable.

Coach Wooden's Method of Building Consistency

After I met with Coach Wooden for the first time, I was struck with the realization that I had never known an individual more clear about his priorities. You cannot be around him for long without feeling the peace and strength that come from holding such well-defined values. That clarity is the result of consistent internal conditioning.

Wooden has combined his great love of poetry, religion, and philosophy with his fundamental belief in repetition to constantly reinforce his most important principles in a very unique way. He has molded the philosophical quotes, verse, and creeds he has gathered over the years into a form that brings his beliefs to life. Every single day, through conversations, writing, presentations, or simply his own disciplined thoughts, Coach Wooden repeats and reinforces these concepts. In this way he continually conditions the ideas into habit. He attaches so much meaning to them that they portray a sense of who he really is. That kind of constant internal conditioning builds tremendous trust and respect in those you work with. Your teammates do not have to question your intent or your values because you consistently reinforce them in words and actions.

One underlying quality of leaders who go beyond success is *unselfishness*. Unselfishness affects every block in the Pyramid of Success, adding immensely to its strength as a structure for legendary leadership. When we are consumed with ourselves, we cannot be truly present for others. This makes it almost impossible to build trust. The positive impact of unselfishness is remarkable. It touches those around us at a very deep, heartfelt level. My wife, Carole, taught me this fundamental principle of leadership shortly after our first daughter, Kelsey, was born.

A Lesson in Love:
The Impact of Unselfishness

Carole and I fell completely in love with Kelsey from the miraculous moment of her birth. In one astonishing moment this beautiful child appeared in our lives, changing and enriching us forever.

After we brought Kelsey home, we settled into the exciting new challenge of parenting. Like all first-time parents, we learned how to care for her as we went along. There was no road map or instruction manual. It was the most wonderful adventure of our lives.

In those first weeks, an indescribable new feeling of love and joy filled our hearts. Carole instinctively seemed to know just what to do to nurture our precious little child. I marveled at her immediate transformation to motherhood.

Whenever I held Kelsey in my arms, I felt about twelve feet off the ground. It was the warmest feeling I had ever known—that is, until she started to cry. Suddenly, I didn't know what to do. I could feel myself tense up as I tried to calm her. But the harder I tried, the more upset she became. I was seized with fear that my little daughter didn't like me. When this happened, inevitably I would rush to find Carole and stiffly hand her the poor sobbing baby. Almost instantly, Carole would manage to comfort Kelsey. I was relieved that Kelsey was once again calm, but started developing a real complex that something was terribly wrong with me as a father!

After a few of these episodes of panic, Carole finally stopped me in my tracks. With Kelsey resting peacefully once again in her arms, she looked directly into my troubled eyes and said, "Why don't you stop thinking about yourself?! When this baby is crying it's because of one of four things. She's either hungry, tired, needs her diaper changed, or she's got gas. It's not about you. Instead of worrying about whether she likes you or not, why don't you just send her love?"

It was as if a giant brick had fallen out of the sky and bopped me right on the head. I had been so consumed with self-pity that I had stopped caring for my child's feelings and had instead thought only of my own. Even though she was less than a month old, Kelsey could sense my selfishness. When I was immersed in myself, I could neither calm nor comfort her.

From that moment forward, whenever Kelsey fussed, I focused on sending her love. It was amazing. She settled down like magic! The feelings of warmth and love I experienced as she found comfort in my arms were so deeply satisfying that they constantly reinforced my focus on sending her love. A new pattern of conditioning was installed that has enriched our connection from that day forward.

Acknowledge Your Teammates' Contributions

As leaders, it is critical that we create an environment where the importance of each member of the team is constantly reinforced. We initiate great momentum when every individual feels a strong sense of unselfish contribution to the higher goals of the team. This must be conditioned consistently throughout the organization.

Early in his career, Coach Wooden had many rules and a few suggestions. Through the years, he gradually switched to having very few rules and many suggestions. One of the most important rules he maintained throughout his career concerned unselfishness. Whenever a teammate threw a key pass, set a tough screen, or hustled to help out on defense, Wooden expected the player who benefited to immediately acknowledge the effort with a nod, a word of thanks, or a thumbs-up sign. This kind of recognition for unselfish teamwork became automatic on UCLA teams. Coach Wooden realized that although only one person puts the ball in the basket, several players contribute to create the opportunity.

The same is true in every facet of business. When a sales representative makes a presentation to an important client, the marketing, operations, administration, production, and research and development teams have all participated in making that presentation possible. It is essential that appreciation and acknowledgment for behind-the-scenes support be conditioned into the heartbeat of your organization. Not only does such recognition fuel even greater positive effort and energy in those around you, it also helps keep you constantly aware of how important your teammates' contributions really are.

By conditioning unselfishness into our organizations and our own hearts, we create a fertile environment for growth and development of several of the 15 Secrets, including self-control, initiative, industriousness, loyalty, friendship, cooperation, and team spirit. Unselfishness is the ultimate connector.

13

Secret #11:

Skill

A t the very heart of the Pyramid of Success we find the eleventh secret of a winning life, *skill*. Its central position is not by chance. Achieving the best of which we are capable and the peace of mind that accompanies such satisfying effort depends heavily on our skill level. The four blocks that rest immediately below and directly beside skill in the pyramid each play essential roles in the development of skill.

Alertness enables us to discover where to fine-tune our present skills and to spot the need to develop new skills. When we combine alertness with *initiative*, we create the opportunity to learn in the most powerful way possible—by doing. Instead of being mildly interested spectators, we become fully involved participants, keenly aware of what is working and what isn't as we take action.

By being alert when we use our initiative, we discover *effective* actions, strategies, and beliefs. We can then *condition* them to become automatic and natural. Through conditioning, we can become master technicians. But, *skill is the combination of technique plus heart.* With repetition we can gain expertise, but only through *inspired repetition* can we access what we are truly capable of and manifest our true skill. Such passion arises when we internalize genuine *team spirit* into our hearts and are driven by a purpose that reaches beyond ourselves.

Skill becomes the foundation on which the next tier of the pyramid is built.

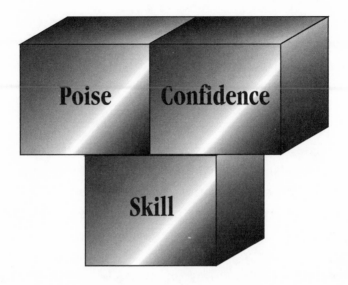

Poise and *confidence* are natural outgrowths of skill, con-ditioned through repetition, and inspired by a true eager-ness to serve others. As our poise and confidence grow, we become much less afraid to take risks. Thus liberated from fear, we once again ignite our alertness and initia-tive, seizing the opportunity to further improve our skill. This cycle of continuous improvement flows naturally when our ultimate goal is not perfection, but peace of mind from knowing we've given the effort to become the best of which we are capable.

Decisiveness: A Critical Contributor to Success

Particularly in today's rapid-fire pace, skill is much more than simply knowing how best to do things. It is the com-bination of deciding specifically what to do, *and doing it quickly.* When I first interviewed John Wooden he put it this way: "Over the years we found several players who were tremendous shooters. Many of them, however, weren't quick enough to get open for any shots, so they didn't help us. There were several other players who were very quick and could create open shots for themselves constantly. They couldn't shoot a lick, though. So they didn't help us much either!"

The knowledge and ability to properly and swiftly execute fundamentals is as critical on the retail floor and in the boardroom as on the basketball court. One of leadership's primary roles is to prepare people to quickly recognize and act on opportunities and on fresh, new ideas.

Creation begins with an idea. Opportunities can stimulate new ideas. But when we wait to respond to opportunities, we limit ourselves. We put ourselves at the effect of circumstances, becoming reactive rather than proactive. It is crucial not only to act on opportunities quickly, but to bring new options about through fostering imagination, resourcefulness, and ingenuity. Just as opportunities give rise to new ideas, so, too, do *ideas create opportunities*. A major challenge for leadership exists today because most people wait for opportunities to approach them or, more commonly, for threats to force them into action. Instead, they should be responding with energy to new ideas. Two examples show how important this is on both an individual and a global level.

Seize Opportunities to Serve Others

Recently, I was in need of new contact lenses and decided to visit a local outlet of one of the world's largest retailers, thinking that its massive buying power would translate into savings on my purchase. As I walked in, there was only one other customer in the optometry area. I smiled at the store clerk, but she made no attempt to acknowledge my presence or offer some idea of how long I might wait before being served. I didn't give much thought to the lack of a greeting, making the assumption that she was simply concentrating on her present customer. I sat down and waited quietly, figuring I would be taken care of quickly with so little activity in the department.

After a few minutes, I began to understand why this huge retailing institution had fallen on such difficult times in the past decade. The clerk left her customer to answer the phone and proceeded to engage in a five-to-ten-minute personal conversation with a friend, talking about her schedule, movies she had seen recently, how slow business had been, and other scattered subjects. It was annoying enough to be kept waiting without some attempt to explain the reasons for the delay, but for her to carry on such a conversation in full view and hearing of customers was ridiculous.

When she finally finished her phone call, she casually asked how she could help me. I explained that I needed new contact lenses and that I had recently moved to the area. She said she couldn't help me without a written report from my previous optometrist. I asked her if we could call my optometrist in San Diego so he could confirm my prescription and fax the necessary paperwork. Her response proved to be the last straw. She said I would have to make the call on my own and the optometrist would have to mail the information to her. "Company policy" did not allow for faxed prescriptions or long-distance calls by customers. I was stunned. I could not believe the lack of flexibility and initiative. She did not make even the slightest effort to ease my dilemma or to set a future appointment. I simply walked out, never to return.

I am certain that, given time to evaluate, the clerk and the company could have come up with better ways to meet my needs. The problem was one not of ability, but of decision and consequent action in the heat of the moment. In business today, it is no longer enough to know what to do. We must do what we know—and do it quickly. This is how we develop capability into skill. I truly believe the clerk knew the right thing to do. She simply didn't do it fast enough. Instead of using her most precious skill, the ability to make spontaneous decisions to support others, she responded in a mechanical and detached manner. She was not prepared to serve. One of leadership's most pressing challenges in the lightning-fast pace of today's business environment is to prepare people to develop the skill of making decisions quickly, clearly, and confidently.

On the surface, the failure of the clerk to react quickly to my needs resulted in the direct loss of a single customer. The impact is magnified, however, if we consider the lost potential of my goodwill and the fact that the actions of one department can easily impact an entire organization. I realize that the clerk's actions could very well have been the exception rather than the rule in that organization. Yet I wondered, as I left, how many others had had similar experiences and also decided to exercise their choice to shop elsewhere.

In business today, it is no longer enough to know what to do. We must do what we know—and do it quickly.

It's extremely revealing to recognize that during the same decade when this mammoth company and other major department stores were suffering huge losses of market share and profits, organizations like Wal-Mart and Nordstrom were growing and prospering at a record pace. The reason is clear: these are companies that constantly encourage and reward their people for using creativity and initiative to quickly respond to customers' needs. They teach their employees the skill of flexible, caring service and have created environments where freedom to make immediate decisions in support of customers is consistently reinforced. They have instilled the belief in their employees that each and every individual is a leader.

A second example demonstrates that even the most technically skilled masters on earth can lose every advantage they have worked years to gain if they fail to respond quickly and decisively to opportunities and ideas.

Stay Ahead with Flexibility of Approach

For centuries, the Swiss have been known around the world for crafting the finest quality timepieces. Until the past fifteen years, they controlled over 75 percent of the watch market worldwide. The precision and delicacy required to manufacture fine analog watches was a major source of national pride and international prestige for the Swiss.

Today, the Swiss possess less than 10 percent of the world market share for watches. Practically overnight the Japanese surged to a dominant position in this multi-billion-dollar industry, on the strength of digital technology. It is a financial coup of epic proportions. What caused this remarkable change?

There is an irony to this startling turn of events that serves as a powerful reminder to leaders to develop the crucial skill of responding quickly to ideas and opportunities. You see, it was the *Swiss* who developed digital watch technology. Their engineers invented the first digital watches and owned the original patents! Yet they viewed digital technology as a fad rather than a revolution, and sold their patents to the Japanese. The skill of Swiss analog watchmakers is still unmatched, but their work is now seen and appreciated mainly by a few collectors and the very wealthy, while the rest of the world wears Japanese digital watches.

Successful companies have instilled the belief in their employees that each and every individual is a leader.

These examples demonstrate the critical importance of *flexibility*—the first of five master skills of winning leadership. A great leader is steadfast in intent, but flexible in approach. This is an essential balance to maintain in the rapidly changing, constantly accelerating world we live in. Solidarity of intent fills your team with the strength of knowing its ultimate purpose and direction. Flexibility of approach allows you to maximize the unique talents of people and to reposition quickly and effectively as conditions change in your organization, industry, or global market. As the team reflects your flexibility in approach, they become highly solution oriented and innovative. They recognize new and different resources they would have missed had they remained rigid in their approach to difficult challenges.

Fun, No Matter How You Slice It

Let's play a little game to illustrate the power of flexibility. I call this game "A Piece of Cake." Here are the instructions.

The figure represents a delicious homemade cake. Using only four straight-line cuts, you are to slice the cake into as many pieces as possible. Go ahead and give it a try now. Draw lines to represent the cuts. Slice away!

How many pieces of cake did you slice—ten, eleven, twelve? If you haven't actually tried the game yet, stop before you read any further and give it a go. Discovery is so much more fun when you're in the game.

If you came up with eleven pieces of cake, good for you. You're a highly efficient—but one-dimensional—thinker. Remember, this is a game about flexibility of approach. Though the diagram looks like a circle, you know it represents a cake. Cakes are three-dimensional. Now do you see a new approach you can use to divide the cake into more pieces? What if your first three cuts were vertical as shown, creating seven pieces, and then for your fourth and final cut, you sliced the cake horizontally (as shown on the next page)? Suddenly, by changing your approach and thinking multidimensionally, you've created fourteen pieces!

Be Open to New Solutions

However, we're not quite through yet! There is more to this fun and interesting game. I have conducted this exercise in many seminars through the years, and figured I knew just about everything there was to know about it. Recently, a participant surprised me by demonstrating once again how the master skill of flexibility can create new results.

$$7 \times 2 = 14$$

Absolutely certain that fourteen pieces was the correct answer, I asked if anyone had sliced the cake into ten pieces. Most hands in the room went up. Then I asked who had divided the cake into eleven pieces, and a few more hands went up. Finally, I asked if anyone had found more than eleven. One young woman raised her hand. Occasionally a participant will come up with the right answer. I love to invite this person up on the stage to demonstrate multidimensional thinking. I was just about to congratulate the woman on her flexibility of approach in arriving at the correct answer of fourteen pieces when I asked, "How many slices did you come up with?" She called out, "Sixteen!"

Immediately I assumed she must have made a mistake. After all, I knew the correct answer. I didn't want to embarrass her in front of everyone, so I said, "That's amazing, but I'll have to look at your solution during the break. I think you might have misunderstood the directions." I then proceeded to demonstrate how to "correctly" slice the cake into fourteen pieces. Once again I enjoyed the surprised reaction from participants.

At the break, the woman came up to show me her sixteen-piece solution. I had almost forgotten about it by that time. I assumed she had used a curved cut, or had inadvertently made five cuts instead of the required four. Very quickly, she proceeded to catch me in the act of inflexible thinking. Using four perfectly straight cuts, she sliced the cake into sixteen pieces, adding a new dimension in approach which I had failed to see in all the times I had played the game before: stacking the pieces between each successive cut! After the first cut, she stacked the two halves on top of each other, then used the second cut to slice the cake into quarters. Gathering the four quarters, she stacked them one on top of the other, and used her third cut to slice the cake into eighths. Next, she stacked all eight pieces and used her final cut to make sixteen. At that moment I knew what it felt like to be a Swiss watchmaker looking at all those Casios!

To be a leader who stimulates true flexibility of approach among your teammates, you must believe deeply that improvements and innovations are constantly available. It is not enough to know this logically in your head. You must feel it in your heart. Otherwise, you can easily fall prey to limited vision, just as the Swiss did when they missed out on the great opportunity their own ideas created to further extend their leadership in the world watch market. You must delight in being surprised by the creativity of your teammates and be constantly open to new possibilities. Flexible leaders treat every person differently, varying their approach to best inspire, reward, and challenge each unique individual. Most important, mastering the skill of flexibility enables leaders to bring out people's heart as well as their talent, so they may pursue their goals and dreams with joy, passion, and inexhaustible energy.

Spark the Discovery Process with Enabling Questioning

The second master skill of winning leadership, *enabling questioning,* is intimately tied to flexibility. The ability to ask questions that uplift, inspire, and empower others is a skill that, in turn, helps us understand the unique qualities of each individual. Through enabling questions we gain the insight to flexibly fine-tune our approach in working with each member of our team so that ultimately all members mesh into a synergistic unit. At the same time, enabling questions catalyze self-discovery by helping us clarify our most important and compelling beliefs.

As human beings we possess an almost magical talent—the ability to envision ourselves in situations and experiences with as much realism and emotion as if they were actually happening. We can surround ourselves instantly with our closest friends and relatives even if they are thousands of miles away. We can vividly remember moments that have touched the very depths of our soul or look forward with amazing detail to events that have not yet occurred. We can feel love, joy, fear, anger, and exaltation simply by tapping into the unlimited resource called our imagination. In psychology the term used to describe this special ability is *full association*. When we are fully associated, every ounce of our body, mind, and spirit is completely involved. We accept total ownership of our experience.

The master skill of enabling questioning is the key to helping ourselves and others enter the enriching world of full association. As leaders develop the skill of asking enabling questions, they accomplish in a moment what they may fail to achieve in hours or even years of commands or dictates: catalyzing others to discover their own reasons to become inspired and committed. Mastering the skill of enabling questioning also demands that *you* become fully associated to your people. The best way to help others become fully associated is to be equally associated with their responses. When you ask an enabling question, its real value is less a product of what you ask than of how you ask. If you ask questions using the correct words, but lacking the empathy and presence that invite full association, you have missed the essence of this special skill. Masters of enabling questions are intensely curious and genuinely interested in each individual with whom they come in contact. They do not ask questions looking for answers they want to hear. They ask enabling questions to *learn*. There are no right or wrong answers to enabling questions—only real answers.

Move from the Head to the Heart

What, then, is an enabling question? Very simply, it is a question that induces full association. It enables an individual to move from the head to the heart. It is enabling because its aim is constructive, allowing its recipient to tap into feelings, thoughts, and experiences that will assist him or her to gain greater inspiration, insight, or resourcefulness. Enabling questions unleash our potential for positive visualization. As we fully associate in response to enabling questions, we suddenly envision new creative solutions, and feel the surge of positive emotion that accompanies the accomplishment of important goals or the knowledge that we have made a difference for our team. Enabling questions create "aha!" answers.

Here is one of several sets of enabling questions I have my seminar participants ask one another during our sessions.

The "Greatest Team" questions

1. **What was (is) the greatest team you've ever been a part of?**

2. **What made (makes) it such a great team?**

3. **How did (do) you feel to be a part of the team?**

4. **What did (do) you contribute to the team?**

5. **What did (do) you receive from the team?**

6. **In a sentence or a phrase, how would you describe the mind-set of the team? Where did that mind-set come from?**

Before participants form pairs and begin this exercise, I have some fun as I explain the difference between fully associated and disassociated participation. Very playfully I say to the class, "If you chose to, you could run through these questions in about thirty seconds. All you'd have to do is answer straight from the top of your head without any real thought. Isn't that the way we ask and answer many questions each day? If you were to zip through these without truly associating, it would go something like this."

Then very quickly, in a dull and lifeless monotone I pretend to be a pair of buddies:

"What was the greatest team you've ever been a part of?"

"My Little League team when I was nine."

"What made it such a great team?"

"Uh . . . it was great."

"How did you feel to be a part of the team?"

"I felt great."

"What did you contribute to the team?"

"Greatness."

"What did you receive from the team?"

"A uniform and a trophy."

"Great."

After we chuckle for a moment, I explain that the goal of these enabling questions is for the participants to imagine that their greatest team is with them, right now. "Hear the voices of your teammates, see their faces, and really feel the emotion of being a part of such a special team. As you ask your partner the questions, you help most by being truly interested. You're about to learn something very special about your teammate that you probably never knew, even though you work with each other every day. By the way, remember that there are all kinds of teams: family, business, sports, church, community, friends. Exploring what helped create your greatest teams will help you bring the same key elements to every team you're a part of today."

Unleashing Potential in Ourselves and Others

This is always an extremely valuable session because participants identify what is most important to them in a team. Lightbulbs go on around the room as everyone learns what specific elements will enrich the team environment for others. When we clarify for ourselves what we've contributed to the greatest teams we've ever been a part of, we immediately recognize that *we can choose to contribute those same gifts now.* In a matter of moments, through these simple questions asked and answered with full association, we have enabled ourselves and enabled others.

It is very important to distinguish between enabling and disabling questions. Both generate association. The difference lies in the emotional direction in which the questions lead. Disabling questions leave us paralyzed with fear and doubt because they focus not on solutions, but on the severity and intensity of the problem. The aim of disabling questions is control—keeping others in check by pulling in the reins.

We have learned from our discussion of vision, intent, and the Pygmalion effect that what we focus on with determination and passion, we ultimately create. Enabling questions lead to solutions—to how we can make things work better. They are energizing, empowering, and incredibly freeing. By helping us to fully associate, they allow us to learn from even our most intense feelings and difficult experiences so that we may grow now and in the future. Enabling questions are aimed at unleashing others' initiative and enthusiasm—leading to ultimate success, which is peace of mind.

A Moment of True Connection

When I first interviewed Coach Wooden, I asked him some enabling questions that led to a moment I will always remember. Well into the interview I asked, "Coach, what was the toughest time you've ever experienced in your life, and what got you through it? What did you learn from that most difficult experience that has helped you ever since?"

He answered, "The most difficult time was when my wife Nellie died, six years ago. She had so much life and love. For a time, I wasn't sure I would get through. I missed her so terribly."

He was quieter now as I asked again, "What is it that got you through?"

"Well, I think it was my children and grandchildren. My family has always been my top priority."

But as he answered, I somehow felt there was something more. His answer had come more from his head than deep in his heart. I asked, "Was there some moment when you found the strength to keep wanting to live?"

To this point his voice had been soft but strong. He was silent for a moment, then spoke in almost a whisper, his voice cracking with emotion. I listened with every ounce of my heart and soul. "There was a time when I didn't think I could go on without Nellie. I was afraid to live without her and afraid to die. But finally, after about a year and a half, I found I no longer feared death. Because I knew that when my time came I would be with her once again, forever. When I stopped fearing dying, I found the strength to keep living."

Enabling questions create the opportunity for such moments of unforgettable connection. As you ask enabling questions, your sincere interest in your teammates shines through. They feel respected and cared about. When people feel that their ideas and opinions count, they usually do! An infectious motivation to contribute begins to build within your organization and within yourself as you master this special skill. In the process, you receive perhaps the greatest gift a leader could ever desire: a growing awareness of the genius, talent, and heart that exists within your own team.

Crystallize Your Dreams with the Tool of Visualization

The third master skill of winning leadership is *visualization*. Many wonderful books and seminars focus on visualization as a key to personal growth, greater financial abundance, and more deeply satisfying relationships. Among the finest are *You'll See It When You Believe It!* by Wayne Dyer, and *Empowerment: The Art of Creating Your Life As You Want It* by the husband and wife team, David Gershon and Gail Straub. Norman Cousins and Dr. Deepak Chopra have demonstrated the tremendous impact of visualization as a tool to promote physical and emotional healing, and James Kouzes and Barry Posner, in *The Leadership Challenge: How to Get Extraordinary Things Done in Organizations,* offer extremely valuable information on the importance of envisioning the future to provide quality leadership.

Throughout these and many other outstanding works, four elements appear most consistently as keys to effective visualization. These four fundamentals, plus one special addition, comprise the core of this third master skill of winning leadership.

The first fundamental of visualization is so important that we have already focused on it numerous times throughout this book. *We must visualize what we want—not what we don't want!* For years without intending to, I led little red-haired Allison on a misguided visualization. Every time I "encouraged" her by saying, "One of these days you're not going to die," she could not help but first see herself in the act of dying once again. When instead we visualized an explosive, exhilarating sprint home in the last twenty-five meters, an entirely new picture was implanted that enabled Allison to access her true potential.

The moment you shift your visualizing from what you don't want to what you do want, you change—physically, mentally, emotionally, and spiritually. The change in results may take time, but the change in the lightness and energy with which you pursue your desired outcome is instantaneous.

The second fundamental of effective visualization is to *see the outcome as if it were already complete*. In other words, look into the future as if it were your present reality. For example, if you want to be thinner and more physically vibrant, visualize yourself looking and feeling terrific at your desired weight. In your visualization it is not that you *want* to be thinner—you already *are* thin.

How to Intensify Your Visualizations

Full association is the key to the third fundamental of effective visualization. As you create a picture of your desired outcome, add immensely to its magnetism by *filling the visualization with vivid detail and rich emotion*. Effective visualization ignites initiative. The more specific, clear, and emotionally enriched your visualization, the more you are drawn to it. Your energy and initiative are directly related to the vividness of your visualization. It is here that you give your ideas real meaning. As you picture what you want with heightened emotion and compelling meaning, you gain absolute certainty that you will do whatever it takes to transform your supercharged vision to reality, because inside yourself the transformation is already complete.

Every great teacher, coach, and leader is a believer in *repetition*—the fourth fundamental of effective visualization. Perhaps no single leadership practice is more essential to repeat constantly than visualization. My youngest daughter, Jenna, brought this principle to life for me. When Jenna first learned to walk, she received direct feedback—just as every other child at this stage does—that told her something wasn't working quite right. She fell again and again. Yet her vision and consequent tenacity were unstoppable. Each stumble to a child learning to walk is not an episode of failure—it is an adventure. Failure is simply a judgment. Because infants have not learned to judge, they have an amazing success rate in learning to walk! They love the adventure and stay with it until walking becomes natural and automatic. Feedback is simply raw material for the next step. We need to reclaim this genius to give full force to our visualizations.

The fifth and final fundamental of effective visualization is not one I have read in books or heard in seminars. Instead, it is something I have observed in others and felt within myself. We give our visualizations their greatest strength when we fill them with people we love and care about. This is the single most powerful way to enliven your visualizations with emotional clout. One of the most moving personal stories of the 1992 Summer Olympics provides a poignant demonstration of the tremendous impact this fundamental of visualization can have.

The Stunning Comeback of Pablo Morales

The oldest member of the 1992 United States Olympic swimming team was 27-year-old Pablo Morales. Eight years earlier at the Los Angeles Olympics, Morales had been the strong favorite to win the gold medal in his specialty, the 100-meter butterfly. He was the world record holder at the time, seemingly at his peak physically, mentally, and emotionally. With the partisan U.S. crowd cheering madly, Morales set a blistering pace in the Olympic finals. With less than ten meters to go, he still led his closest rival, West Germany's Michael Gross, by a couple of feet. But as they drove together toward the finish, Gross seemed to gain new strength while Morales tightened up badly. In the final two strokes, the German powered past Morales to win the gold medal and establish a new world record.

It was a bitterly disappointing defeat for Morales. The Olympics come only once every four years, and it was tough for him to imagine hanging on for a second shot at the gold in Seoul, Korea, in 1988. By then he would be twenty-three and have graduated from Stanford. He'd be out in the real world, beginning a career or starting graduate school. Four more years of 5 A.M. workouts, pushing his body and mind to the limit, seemed nearly incomprehensible.

Yet when the 1988 Olympic Trials began, there was Morales once again. Going into the trials, he had regained the world record, becoming the only man to swim the 100-meter butterfly in less than fifty-three seconds. He had endured the disappointment of 1984 and emerged as the huge favorite to earn another Olympic berth.

It was not to be. In a shocking upset, Pablo finished third in the finals of the Olympic Trials, failing even to qualify for the U.S. team. He would not be going to Seoul. The gold medal would be won by Anthony Nesty of Surinam, with a time slower than Morales' world record.

Morales could not rewrite his personal Olympic history, but he was deeply appreciative of the opportunities he had been given to compete at the most elite level. He retired from swimming with several NCAA individual championships, his world record still intact, and many wonderful friendships he had developed as he pursued his dreams. When he began law school at Cornell University, his swimming story seemed complete.

But even faded dreams can reignite when we enhance our visualizations with images of those we deeply care about. In 1991, more than two years since he had officially retired from the sport, Morales found himself back in the pool, rededicated to his Olympic dream.

That summer his mother had lost a fierce battle with cancer. She had been Pablo's dearest friend and greatest fan, giving him endless love and encouragement through the glory and the pain. They adored one another. Just before she passed away, Pablo made the decision to try one more time for his Olympic dream—dedicating this final comeback to her.

The Fuel That Never Quits

Throughout his long climb back to competitive form, Morales kept his mother's memory alive. Every time he felt as if his body could take no more, he pictured his mom cheering and filled with pride. His visualization gave him the strength to keep going. At the Olympic Trials, and again at the Olympics themselves in Barcelona, Morales' final preparation before his race was a moment of quiet visualization. In silence, he filled his mind and heart with the image of his mom bursting with joy. Then he stepped onto the starting blocks, ready to give his finest effort.

In the Olympic final with ten meters to go, just as eight years before, Pablo found himself slightly ahead with the field closing in. Once again he could feel his muscles tightening as he struggled to hang on. This time, though, he was swimming for so much more. He put his head down and drove for the wall with every ounce of strength he had left. The touch was incredibly close. Before he turned to look up at the results, he covered his eyes with his hands for just a moment, feeling all he had given to realize this vision for his mom and himself. Then a smile of deep satisfaction lit up his face. He had done it! He had won the gold medal. By infusing his visualization with a person he loved so dearly, he had broken through his ultimate barrier.

The 5 Fundamentals
of Effective Visualization

1. **Visualize what you want—not what you don't want!**

2. **See the outcome as if it is already complete.**

3. **Fill your visualization with vivid detail and rich emotion.**

4. **Repeat your visualization consistently.**

5. **Infuse your visualizations with people you love and care about.**

These fundamentals are essential skills to develop in ourselves and others. In nearly every endeavor of real magnitude, there are times when it is difficult to maintain faith in our vision. It is easy to doubt and to become so overwhelmed with short-term feedback that we begin to lose sight of our ultimate destination. A primary leadership skill is to embrace feedback as valuable learning material, using new information to further clarify and illuminate our visualizations.

Activate Your Faith by Letting Go

Coach Wooden constantly demonstrated the impact the fourth master skill of winning leadership—*letting go*—had on all those he worked with. Though he was extremely disciplined and believed strongly in structure and meticulous preparation, perhaps no coach has ever had more faith in his players, assistant coaches, and himself. A deeply spiritual man, Wooden's faith in God was complete. This allowed him to balance genuine humility with solid belief in himself. He never chased perfection because he believed it to be the sole domain of God. Nor did he dwell on mistakes or disappointments. Instead, he sought to give his utmost effort to become the best of which he was capable. He had complete faith that this was possible for everyone. Letting go is a product of faith. This faith enabled him to feel complete today, yet strive for more tomorrow.

Coach Wooden would be the first to tell you that he was a practice coach. He believed that 95 percent of his job was performed on the practice floor and in the hours he' spent each day preparing for practice in his tiny UCLA office. Once the game began, the ball was in the players' hands. He made a few subtle adjustments and watched for important substitutions, but by and large he put his faith in his players to carry out their responsibilities and execute the fundamentals properly. By letting go and allowing his players to carry out their training, he filled them with tremendous confidence and determination. It became natural and automatic for them to accept full accountability for their contributions to the overall team effort.

Letting go is a product of faith. Faith enables you to feel complete today, yet strive for more tomorrow.

In his personal life, Coach Wooden provided perhaps an even stronger example of this master skill of letting go. Throughout his coaching career, he managed to let go of the rigors and pressures of his work and to truly enjoy his family. Together, he and Nellie celebrated the countless joys of raising their children and filling their home with warmth and love. When he returned to the basketball court each day, he was a shining example of balance and simple values. He gave his players a beautiful model of peace of mind. Learning to let go appropriately is the key to living in harmony with your priorities and providing the kind of leadership that brings out the best in everyone.

Taking the Lone Pine Challenge

Recently, on one of my frequent visits to the little town of Klamath Falls, Oregon, for my work with Cell Tech, I enjoyed one of those startling "aha!" experiences that helped crystallize my thoughts about the master skills of winning leadership. From my very first trip to the Klamath basin, I was drawn to the sight of a striking natural landmark—a single tree that stands completely alone at the top of a large hill at the edge of town. The tree seems to climb straight up out of the rock. An avid runner, I was immediately attracted to this lone pine. I became determined to run to the top of the hill and stand beside it.

To my delight, I found that there are several rough trails leading to the great tree. Ever since that first visit, it has become my ritual on every trip to Klamath to run to Lone Pine, exploring a new path whenever I can. I find great satisfaction in the physical challenge of running up the steep grade without succumbing to the urge to stop and walk or rest along the way. A magnificent view of Mount Shasta and a wonderful, refreshing breeze await me as special rewards when I reach my goal.

As I set out early in the morning on my most recent adventure to Lone Pine, I was struck by what a perfect metaphor this climb represents for the journey of leadership. All five master skills play important roles at crucial points along the way.

The moment I left my hotel, I looked up to see Lone Pine looming regally over the basin. From a dis-

tance, my goal looked deceivingly simple. The great ponderosa pine stood in clear view, almost as if I could reach
out and touch it. As I approached the base of the hill I
took one final moment to stare at the tree in silence, lock-
ing in the vision before I began the rugged climb.

As soon as I actually began to run, however, something fascinating happened. The goal disappeared from
sight! No longer was there a straight line of vision
between my objective and me. Instead, all I could see
was about one hundred yards of rocky trail rising steeply
in front of me. After only ten minutes or so, my legs were
already beginning to burn. Suddenly, the effort required
to reach my goal had become painfully real.

Mobilize Your Visualization, Flexibility, and Enabling Questioning

As I kept running up, up, up, I realized that the only
place I could see my goal now was in my own imagination. This early part of the run, after the initial freshness of
my first half mile or so had worn off, was the toughest
part of the effort. It was here that the trail seemed most
intense and difficult. Even more oppressive than the physical challenge was the thought I kept trying to push out of
my mind about what a long way I had to go. When I
focused on what I didn't want, my legs burned even more
fiercely and I felt my heart racing even faster from the
effects of the altitude.

This is where it's easy to give in to temptation and
say, "Oh, heck, I'll just walk." It is at points like this
where visualization must be strongest.

Just when my legs felt like they would explode, the trail led into a little meadow where the grade finally eased. My breathing slowed and I felt my body recover just a bit. The reprieve was only momentary, however, for as soon as I began to feel my second wind, a new challenge appeared. The power of my visualization had carried me through so far, but now the master skill of flexibility would be called upon.

In the next few minutes, I came to a couple of forks in the trail. Which way should I go? There were no signs, no maps to assure me that I was making the right choices. All the trails on the hill twisted and turned so often, there was no way of knowing where they'd end up. I simply had to decide quickly and be flexible enough to change my approach if I felt I was moving away from my goal. I chose the trail that seemed to head most directly toward where I hoped the tree was, knowing full well it could lead almost anywhere. Soon the grade steepened once again. Huffing and puffing, I kept on climbing.

I had to decide quickly and be flexible enough to change my approach if I felt I was moving away from my goal.

As the pain increased, it was easy for my mind to play tricks. Here, the master skill of enabling questioning became essential. With only an idea—the visualization of my goal—to guide me, it was easy to fall into the pattern of asking myself disabling questions such as, Did I go the wrong way? or Why did I make that last turn? Am I ever going to get there? For a moment I surrounded myself with HIQs and HAQs!

Then I shifted my focus by asking myself enabling questions like, How will I most enjoy the rest of my climb? What gifts can I discover around me by using all my senses? How will I feel when I reach the top and look out at the incredible beauty? I immediately felt lighter, stronger, and revitalized. It was a striking example of the power of enabling questions to help us discover resources and energy when we need them the most.

Savor Moments of Celebration

Finally, after forty-five minutes of intense uphill running, I came around a little turn. There before me, no more than one hundred yards away, was Lone Pine! Suddenly I felt like Carl Lewis. With newfound strength and purpose I sprinted the final few yards. I refused to stop until I had actually touched the great pine. With a huge grin on my face I raised both arms in triumph. As sweat poured off me, I stood silently beside this magnificent ponderosa and looked out toward Mount Shasta and the Klamath basin, basking in the serenity and joy I felt.

I stayed there for quite some time, allowing myself to enjoy the gifts we receive when we apply the master skill of letting go. So often in the past, I had hurried off after I reached a goal, not allowing myself to let go and celebrate the moment. This time, however, I realized that I had come here for far more than simply to run to the top and immediately zip back down. I had come to stretch, to grow, and to learn. There was a full and rich experience here for me if I gave myself the chance to discover and truly enjoy it. Letting go and allowing myself to receive and to celebrate was an important part of that complete experience.

A hawk put on a dazzling display for me as it soared against the crystalline sky. I closed my eyes and spent some quiet moments envisioning my wife and children. As I visualized them one at a time, I thought about how I could express even more love and appreciation to each of them. I felt them with me, in my heart, lifting my spirit. I let the fresh breeze cool me and listened to its soft music blowing through the brush. For a few peaceful moments, I reconnected with the special inner satisfaction that comes from persevering and refusing to quit.

Our most important challenges personally, organizationally, and globally are very much like my climb to Lone Pine. When we begin, our goals can seem very simple and within reach. We are filled with fresh enthusiasm. But as we begin to climb, we often meet obstacles and face choices we had no way of anticipating. We must make decisions quickly and carry out the fundamentals we have practiced diligently. As we make these decisions, we must be alert to what we are learning along the way, and flexibly change our approach when we spot a new possibility or find ourselves drifting away from our goals. The vision that seemed so close when we began may fade from view, obscured by the immensity of the difficulties surrounding us. In the midst of so much distraction, we must call on our ability to visualize what we truly want. We can easily fall prey to doubt and fear if we begin to ask disabling rather than enabling questions. If we do persevere and reach our goal, we will feel a burst of new energy we thought we had used up. And when we reach our goal, as well as every step along the way, we have the opportunity to let go of unnecessary ego, of conditioning that no longer serves us, and of our tendency to forget to celebrate each precious moment.

Inspire Others by Expressing Yourself with Dimension

As I started back down the hill I realized how crucial the final master skill of winning leadership—*expressing yourself with dimension*—is to elevating your team to its true potential. As a leader, one of your most important goals is to inspire your team to feel the same kind of strength and energy I felt when Lone Pine suddenly appeared before me with only a hundred yards to go. Mastering the skill of expressing yourself with dimension is the key to catalyzing this kind of motivation and vision when the goal disappears from view. It is during the climb, when your legs are burning and you begin to wonder if you're ever going to make it, that leadership must step forward. Every business, family, and team faces these periods of intense effort, when dreams and vision can begin to fade. By expressing yourself with dimension, you provide the color and detail that can bring others' visualizations to life when they are needed most.

Expressing yourself with dimension means you combine head and heart when you communicate with others. It demands that you be completely present. There is perhaps no greater challenge for many leaders than this fifth master skill. They may genuinely care about people and sincerely want to share their vision. But they have great difficulty in expressing themselves with the dimension that touches people's hearts and fires their imaginations.

Some leaders try to communicate purely from a position of authority. But strength without vulnerability is dominating and restrictive. Rather than feeling encouraged, people feel intimidated and overwhelmed. Such communication does not stimulate the development of a shared team vision, drawing together each individual's personal goals. Instead, leaders who communicate strictly from a position of power seek to control and to generate compliance and subservience. The greatest fear of such a leader is to be found wrong. As a result, an environment is created where blame flourishes and loyalty is temporary and self-serving. The ultimate aim of such communication is to create followers, not leaders.

On the other hand, an individual who communicates strictly from a place of vulnerability generates feelings of pity and doubt rather than loyalty and confidence. When communication is delivered solely from this perspective, people develop a sense of duty, driven more by a desire to avoid guilt than by enthusiasm and passion.

When you express yourself with dimension, you combine strength and vulnerability, head and heart. You are willing to express your joy and your sadness. You touch hearts with your humanness, yet inspire great confidence in your leadership through the strength of your vision. People in your organization sense that you believe deeply in yourself, and at the same time they know how unstoppable your belief is in them. They feel truly important.

The five master skills of winning leadership all share the same ultimate objective. They enable you as a leader to bring out the heart in each member of your team. Heart is the mortar that cements each of the fifteen secrets together into a synergistic system of leadership and personal growth.

14

Secret #12:

Team Spirit

*It's amazing how much can be accomplished
when no one cares who gets the credit.*

—JOHN WOODEN

This quote from Coach Wooden burst into my
mind as I watched the last seconds of the deciding game of the 1993 NBA Championship
between the Chicago Bulls and the Phoenix Suns. Chicago
was set to inbound the ball, down by two points with
only thirteen seconds left to play. Everyone in Chicago
Stadium looked for the Bulls to go to the incomparable

Michael Jordan for the final shot. Never in the history of the sport has there been a greater offensive player than Jordan. He had carried the Bulls to two consecutive World Championships on the strength of his amazing ability and unrelenting desire. True to form, for most of this critical game he had seemed poised to lead them to a third straight title. Yet in the fourth quarter his Bulls teammates had gone stone cold. They had scored only nine points in the period—all by Jordan—and had watched their lead steadily disintegrate. Now it was down to this final play.

The inbound pass came to Jordan, who was quickly double-teamed by the Suns. Instantly he snapped a pass to his teammate, Scottie Pippen, who drove down the center of the court. With Phoenix determined to deny Jordan the last shot, everyone's focus now turned to Pippen. Surely he would take the shot. As he approached the top of the key, he drew two Suns players to him. Suddenly, he zipped a perfect pass to Horace Grant, who had been left completely alone under the basket. The sure layup would tie the game and send it into overtime. After the dismal fourth quarter, that seemed like a huge reprieve for the reeling Bulls.

As the ball sped toward Grant, Phoenix guard Danny Ainge instinctively left his man and flew at the big Bulls forward, desperately trying to disrupt his wide-open shot. Out of the corner of his eye, Grant spotted Ainge lunging toward him and instantly made an extraordinary decision. In one lightning-quick motion, Grant caught the ball from Pippen and immediately volleyballed a perfect pass to Ainge's man, John Paxson, now standing completely free at the three-point line.

With Phoenix determined to deny Jordan the last shot, everyone's focus now turned to Pippen.

Without hesitation, Paxson fired. Time seemed to stand still as the ball spun toward the basket. There was a moment of eerie silence as every eye in the stadium stared in unison at the high-arching shot. Swish! The crowd erupted as the ball found its mark perfectly, nestling gently in the net. The Suns were unable to answer in the final four seconds. The Bulls had won their third consecutive NBA Championship.

The Power of Putting the Team First

I'm certain Coach Wooden was smiling as he watched that final play because it was such a perfect example of the kind of unselfish teamwork he constantly demanded of his players. To Wooden, true *team spirit* was the manifestation of unselfishness in its purest form: genuine consideration for others. In that brilliant nine-second flurry, four different players had touched the ball, each completely intent on working together rather than gaining personal glory. It was magic.

During this sequence of exquisite team play, Michael Jordan had readily accepted his role as a decoy because it meant someone on his team would be open for a good shot. Scottie Pippen eagerly pulled the pressure to himself to create even more opportunity for the team. Horace Grant's effort especially demonstrated unselfish team spirit. Standing completely free under the basket, he had the opportunity to be the star, to sink the critical shot that would tie the game and send it into overtime. Instead, he chose to put the team first. His pass to John Paxson was as spiritually ennobling as it was perfectly executed. Grant's bullet pass was more than an important assist. It was a dynamic transfer of his complete faith and trust. As the ball fell through the net, I couldn't help but think that Jordan's, Pippen's, and finally Grant's unselfishness were the keys to Paxson's total confidence in that pivotal moment when the season hung in the balance.

Throughout his career, Coach Wooden prepared his players to look for important opportunities to put the team first, both on the basketball court and in life. To him, true consideration for others meant "a complete eagerness to lose oneself in the team, for the good of the team." This eagerness is derived from absolute certainty that you will do whatever it takes to support your team. More than the zone press, more than the fast-break style of play he taught, this unselfish team spirit was the most important trademark of Coach Wooden's teams. It meant that his players made the unselfish pass a little sooner, set screens and picks with extra resolve, and dedicated themselves completely to exceptional conditioning. They eagerly concentrated on the small things that made the biggest difference. As he put it, "Success accompanies attention to little details. It is this that makes for the difference between champion and near champion."

How can you instill such extraordinary team spirit in yourself and others? What is the leadership formula for fostering genuine consideration for others? Three key factors play primary roles in your effectiveness as a builder of outstanding team spirit.

How to Infuse a Sense of Cooperation

Team spirit begins with *selection*. As you bring people into teams, look for individuals who place their highest goals and aspirations in a team context. For example, John Wooden's two great superstar centers—Kareem Abdul-Jabbar and Bill Walton—were very different in personality and physical strengths. Yet in one way they were remarkably similar. Each drove himself to be the very best he could be—always in relation to the team. It was no coincidence that these two Hall of Famers were extraordinary passers and defenders as well as shooters and rebounders. They developed these less glamorous abilities as a direct result of their uncompromising team spirit. They were not motivated by personal statistics or awards. The credit they truly valued was credit for the team.

A second key to developing team spirit centers around the way you *acknowledge and discipline* those you lead. True consideration for others requires keen observation and heightened alertness. It is easy to acknowledge individuals who are in the spotlight. Outstanding leaders, however, look deeper for the subtle, sometimes hidden efforts that make successful results possible. Coach Wooden was extremely consistent in acknowledging behind-the-scenes contributors. He was particularly cognizant of praising the unsung heroes publicly. He knew that the media would give considerable ink to the stars, and he sought to create a greater balance of appreciation for his less visible players. He held steadfastly to the belief that "the greatest element in stardom is the rest of the team." He also knew how much it meant to the team for his top players to adopt this same unselfish view. When he complimented his star players, both privately and publicly, it was rarely for the more obvious statistics they piled up. Instead, it was most often for the little extras they gave to support the team, from playing tenacious defense, to providing exemplary leadership, to hustling without the ball. In this way he constantly rewarded the effort above the result.

> **Outstanding leaders look deeper for the subtle, sometimes hidden efforts that make successful results possible.**

His insistence on unselfishness was also the single most important focus for Coach Wooden's discipline. He dealt with mistakes in execution with simple, direct instruction. Selfish acts or decisions, however, were cause for his most severe disciplinary action because, he believed, his athletes' greatest privilege was to practice, and next greatest was to play in the games. If a player put himself above the team, Coach Wooden would remove these privileges until an absolute commitment to team play was firmly reestablished. Once the point was taken, he welcomed the player back without hesitation. As he put it, "Occasionally, the bench is a coach's best friend." Through this consistent reinforcement of the principle of team spirit, his players knew exactly what was expected of them.

The Strongest Factor in Building a Team

The third and ultimately most powerful ingredient in a complete recipe for boundless team spirit is your own example of consideration for others. When you meet Coach Wooden, you discover what genuine consideration is. He speaks softly and exudes gentleness, yet his strength and character shine through instantly. You immediately sense that his motives are not to force a reaction for selfish purposes, but rather to give. Because all people are important to him, he is considerate to all. Such consideration for others is not a "technique." It is a genuineness of spirit.

Whether on the practice floor, during games, or away from basketball, Coach Wooden treated his players with dignity and respect. These are two of the most essential elements that underlie consideration for others. Even when he felt compelled to bench a player or ask him to leave the practice floor, he welcomed him back without reservation when he had completed the restriction. Wooden believed not only in his players' athletic ability, he believed resolutely in their learning ability.

Dignity and respect are two of the most essential elements that underlie consideration for others.

His players saw the same kind of dignity and respect from Coach Wooden in the way he worked with the assistant coaches, trainers, and managers. He sought their advice regularly and listened intently to their recommendations and insights. Most important, he often acted upon their counsel. Over the years, many of his assistants went on to become highly successful head coaches in their own right. He was extremely proud of them, and considered himself very fortunate to have had the opportunity to work with them. They never stopped being a part of his team.

His personal example of devotion to family was perhaps the single greatest demonstration of team spirit he provided to his players. They saw how close-knit and connected the Wooden family was, and realized that their coach walked his talk about building *his* most important team through the same principles and consideration for others he emphasized daily on the basketball court.

As a leader, your own example of genuine consideration for others is the most powerful quality you possess to develop team spirit in your team. This spirit exists within all of us. Its presence is one of the key reasons that in any moment every individual has the potential to step forward and assume a leadership role.

When you come from a place of true team spirit, you influence those around you at the deepest level. I will never forget an experience that demonstrated the remarkable impact this principle has to help others overcome immense obstacles and to reconnect with their true intent.

One Last-Ditch Attempt

Several years ago I received a disturbing call from an old friend I hadn't spoken with in years. He told me that a mutual friend, one of my closest buddies from high school, had become addicted to cocaine. Tom's life was sinking rapidly in the quicksand of paranoia. To pay for his drug habit, he had become embroiled in a shady financial deal that had apparently angered some local heavies. They threatened him repeatedly. He lived in constant fear, refusing to sleep without a gun by his side.

Virtually every aspect of his world was falling apart. The woman with whom he had been head-over-heels in love broke up with him, sinking his spirit even deeper into self-pity and despair. The small business he co-owned with Roland (the friend who had called me that day) and one of his brothers was beginning to suffer as well. Exhausted from lack of sleep and deeply disturbed by apprehension and pain, he was no longer pulling his weight. He had begun to see cocaine as his only escape.

Tom came from a home that was filled with warmth, but as he fell deeper into addiction, he pulled himself further and further away from his family. He had

243

six brothers and sisters, each very different in personality and interests but all united in the love and closeness they felt toward one another. He didn't just respect his parents; he adored them. The thought of their learning of his cocaine dependency was terrifying to Tom. When he spoke to them, he pretended everything was fine. But deep down, he was desperately afraid of losing their love. The shame and guilt he felt from hiding his problem and living a constant lie was tearing him apart.

Roland had called that day to ask me to participate in an "intervention" for Tom. I had never heard of this before. He told me that an intervention is a proactive attempt by those who care deeply about someone with a serious drug or alcohol problem to break through denial and avoidance and confront the problem head-on. In an intervention, all the people who love and care about the person come together at once to meet with him face-to-face and encourage him to get help. Most often this is a last resort.

When Roland and Brian, Tom's brother, decided to call for the intervention, they knew it was a gamble. They had to devise a way to get him to the meeting without letting him know anything about it. It was like a surprise party with a deadly serious purpose. They had no idea how he would react when he walked into that room.

The Team Assembles

Most often, the success of an intervention depends on the level of connection the individual feels to the people in the room. Respect, friendship, and love must combine to create an emotional crowbar strong enough to pry the addict free from the drug's death grip.

The twenty of us who gathered in that room had come for one united purpose. All of us loved Tom and were willing to risk our friendship to help him.

I hadn't seen much of him in about seven years, but we had a relationship that would always remain special. He had a heart of gold and a smile that could light up any room. When we were growing up, we all looked up to him because he was such an outstanding natural athlete. As long as I could remember, he could outrun, outjump, and outperform us in almost every sport. He had been the star of our high school football team and was elected captain as much for his leadership and team spirit as for his athletic ability. He was always there for his teammates. Every one of us would have run through a wall for him.

All of us loved Tom and were willing to risk our friendship to help him.

As I looked around that evening, I saw many familiar faces. Each of us had moved in different directions over the years, but we had come together now to support our friend. It was great to see his brothers and sisters again, even under these difficult circumstances. I knew how much they loved their brother. His mom and dad were there too. It would be a shock for Tom to see them there. He had tried so hard to hide the truth from them.

We waited nervously for a few minutes until Tom's brother, Brian, stepped into the room. He informed us that Tom and Roland would arrive in just a moment. He explained that they had told Tom they had set up a meeting with a counselor and a couple of recovering cocaine addicts. They had had to push very hard to convince Tom to come.

Then Brian gave us the game plan for the intervention. The chairs had been set up in a circle so Tom could see each of us. He would undoubtedly be embarrassed and shocked when he saw that all of us knew of his drug problem. There was a real chance that he would push us away. We all would have an opportunity to say something to Tom. Brian asked that we simply speak from our hearts and say whatever we felt was important to say. More than anything else, Tom needed to know that we loved him and believed in him. Our greatest hope was that he would agree to enter the residential drug rehabilitation program right then and there.

Face to Face with the Truth

Our hearts were pounding as Tom entered the room. Roland, his oldest and closest friend, spoke first. He explained the purpose of the intervention to Tom, and how he and Brian had struggled back and forth before finally deciding to go through with it. He talked about how much Tom's friendship meant to him and how much he loved him. He was afraid to lose that love. But now Tom's health meant more. Roland recalled how he had lost his two-year-old son in a terrible drowning accident. There was nothing he could do to bring his child back. He could not bear the thought of standing by helplessly as his best friend now drowned himself in cocaine.

Tears welled up in our eyes as Roland spoke. The emotion in the room was unbelievably intense. One by one, each of us searched for the words to express our true feelings about our friend. Through it all, Tom remained stiff and impassive. He said very little. He neither smiled nor cried. As we spoke, he turned his eyes toward us, then seemed to go into and out of focus. It felt at times like he was looking through us—as if we weren't really there. I could see his jawbone grinding as he struggled to keep control of his rising emotions.

His mom and dad sat directly across the circle from him, saying nothing as they listened intently to each person speak. Tears streamed down his mom's cheeks. Tom tried to block his parents out, refusing to look in their direction.

Finally, when one of the friends he had often partied with spoke up, Tom lashed out. His head shaking in disgust, he decried the hypocrisy he felt from people who were telling him to quit cocaine while they were users themselves. There was controlled fury in his voice, more icily combative than brazenly defiant.

At that point it seemed that the intervention was going to fail. For a few moments we ceased being a connected team driven by the singular purpose of helping our friend. As the atmosphere turned from united support and concern to isolated blame and defensiveness, I began to doubt if we were going to get anywhere.

But the power of a human being who comes from a place of sincere team spirit is unshakable. When consideration for others becomes more important than your own ego, your spirit cuts through defensiveness and reaches straight into others' hearts.

The power of a human being who comes from a place of sincere team spirit is unshakable.

Just as the intervention wavered on the brink of disaster, Tom's mother stepped forward and quietly brought all of us back to our true purpose. Blinking away her tears, she strode across the circle to Tom and reached out to him. As she looked into his eyes she spoke softly, her voice trembling with emotion.

"I don't care what's happened before. I don't know why this has happened. I just want you to be you again. All I want is to have my Tom back."

When she finished speaking, Tom finally looked into her eyes, so filled with love and pain, and threw his arms around her, burying his face in her shoulder and squeezing her close. As they stood together, hugging and crying, his dad rose and walked over to them. Then, one by one, we all joined them in an embrace that expressed our feelings far more eloquently than any words. It was a moment of sublime connection. The message of our deeply unified team spirit more than touched Tom's heart—it grabbed it and shook it back to life.

As we held each other, Tom committed to enter the rehabilitation program immediately. He was true to his word. He has been free of cocaine ever since.

Break Through with Love and Caring

Our intervention team that evening exemplified the remarkable impact we make when we are truly committed to the Wooden definition of team spirit—genuine eagerness to dedicate oneself to the good of the team. When all members of a team come together for this purpose, they automatically accept full responsibility for their contributions to the total team effort. In organizations alive with such unselfish team spirit, each individual is eager to sacrifice personal interests or glory for the welfare of the greater whole. In other words, the team comes first.

We were a remarkable team that evening for another important reason. Each and every one of us openly expressed the love, respect, and appreciation we felt for our friend. We held nothing back. We shared our hearts with Tom because we cared deeply about him. But in doing so something extraordinary happened within each of us. As we told Tom how much we cared about him, we released our own feelings of pain, fear, and incompleteness. Though we had come to help free Tom from his dependence on drugs, we discovered a fundamental truth about freeing ourselves as well: The love we fail to share is the only pain we live with. As a leader, the impact of sharing your love and appreciation with your team is perhaps the most inspiring and motivating action you can take. This is proactive consideration for others which enables you to build your team and every person you work with. You become a dynamic, positive Pygmalion, igniting loyalty, energy, and initiative. As powerful as acknowledgment is to others, it is even more empowering within yourself. It is the foundational secret to taking care of the "team" inside of you.

The love we fail to share is the only pain we live with.

As consideration for others builds, our need to compare ourselves to others fades. In many businesses, there is a conscious effort on the part of leadership to generate internal competition by comparing individual performance among salespeople, divisions, or locations. When this becomes the focus for motivation within an organization, the goal shifts from giving the best of which you're capable to beating your teammates. A climate of divisiveness and withheld information is established because sharing actions, strategies, and beliefs that are working well for you might allow others to surpass your performance.

Everyone Is Important

The antidote is to replace disabling comparison with enabling consolidation. To consolidate means to unite into a single whole. As a swim coach, some of my most vivid memories were of relay teammates cheering madly together as the anchor leg drove for home. Watching them lean toward the water, completely focused on infusing their teammates with energy and support, was incredibly inspiring. All had given their full-out efforts just moments before. But now, their own physical exhaustion could not hold a candle to their desire to encourage their teammate.

When the relay was through, regardless of who touched the wall first, the athletes were drawn to one another, connecting in an embrace of genuine appreciation. In a relay, no one cares who goes faster than whom. *Everyone is important.* The greatest individual relay performance in history is worth nothing without the rest of the team. It is the total team effort that matters.

Team spirit, like real love, is unconditional. If you reserve your consideration for others to a select few who agree with your philosophy and strategy, you will build barriers rather than bridges throughout your organization, whether it is your business or your family. True consideration requires faith, and where there is faith there can be no blame, no prejudice, and no exclusion. When you live with genuine consideration for others, you value their differences rather than fearing them.

On an individual level, adopting a deeper level of consideration for others assists you to build stronger relationships even with the people you suspect were put on earth to challenge your team spirit! In my experience, no single factor is more responsible for people leaving a team than having a teammate they simply can't get along with. Most often, they've sought both consciously and subconsciously to avoid this other person until one of the two decides to leave the team, or until they explode in confrontation.

The challenge is not what these ill feelings do to your rival; it is the effect they have on you and all those you come in contact with. Antagonistic thoughts can become cancerous within you, gradually eating away your joy, your energy, and your peace of mind. Often, you express your distaste for the individual subconsciously, by being short or impatient with those you love and care about. You begin to concentrate so determinedly on what you don't like in this individual that you become an increasingly critical *negative* Pygmalion. As bitterness and jealousy infect your spirit, you can become obsessed with having to be "right" rather than looking for win-win solutions. You stop listening. All the while, the target of your distaste may be largely unaffected.

When you live with genuine consideration for others, you value their differences rather than fearing them.

When we accept the responsibility of true team spirit, we hold the key to letting go of these parasitic feelings. In Chapter 13, we learned about the fourth master skill of winning leadership: letting go. We cannot truly let go until we become completely committed to genuine consideration for others. When we learn to accept the individuals we are certain God put here to "test" us and to work together as teammates instead, our own ability to lead and to move closer to the best of which we're capable will soar. Dr. Wayne Dyer, author of several marvelous books on personal and spiritual development including *Your Erroneous Zones* and *You'll See It When You Believe It!* has said, "To forgive, you must first have blamed." When we become full-out team players, eager to let go of our own ego and selfish interests for the good of the team, we find a key to move beyond the need to blame. This internal transformation begins by looking at others in the context of a team we truly care about and of which each member is a vital part.

Define—and Redefine—Your Team

During my years at Lynden Air Freight, I found myself constantly at odds with our vice president of operations. We had very different approaches to business and leadership. When problems and challenges arose, I tended to move immediately into solution, looking for the opportunity inherent in any crisis. He, on the other hand, focused much more on detailed analysis of the problem itself. Though our offices were directly next door, the thin wall that separated us might as well have been the Iron

Curtain. The only time we spent together was in meetings when it was absolutely necessary.

The majority of the company's employees were our responsibility. Though we pretended that our relationship was solid, our differences were glaringly obvious to everyone. Our aversion for each other trickled down throughout the entire company. By rejecting rather than embracing our differences, we erected a huge barrier that split our organization into opposing camps. It became far more important to prove that one division was right and the other wrong than to join together for common goals.

For months we talked about the need to come together as a team. But we failed to walk our talk. Finally, one simple question triggered a fundamental change. The question was "Who is the team?" It is a foundational question to ask consciously and often in your organization. In the midst of our conflicts over style and approach, we had come to view our divisions as separate teams. We completely lost sight of the fact that we were all one team. We needed each other's support and excellence far more than we needed to be "right." This question jolted us from our shortsightedness and provided a powerful reality check. We finally recognized at a fundamental level that we were part of the same connected team. In the context of this bigger team, subgrouping and fractionalizing served no constructive purpose.

We had fostered the separateness only to bolster our own egos and to promote our special interests. When we realized who the real team was, we saw how critical it was to everyone to move from grudging tolerance to genuine consideration and support.

The vice president of operations and I sat down together and truly talked for the first time. In a half hour as genuine teammates we understood more about each other than we had allowed ourselves to learn in a year as adversaries. I was amazed at how much we had in common. We had been so focused on our differences in style that we had failed to see the important values and objectives we shared. Most of all, I saw how deeply he cared about his team. He was just as dedicated as I was to building a successful company, one that would provide exciting and fulfilling futures for our employees.

"Who is the team?" is a foundational question to ask consciously and often in your organization.

The new respect and consideration we felt toward each other had a striking effect on the company as a whole. We no longer accepted the inevitability of constant rifts between sales and operations. We began to understand that our most important customers were our own teammates. By envisioning our divisions in the context of our larger, connected team, we moved from ego to "we go!"

On a much larger scale, team spirit—genuine consideration for others—is the great hope for us all. More wars and more deaths have resulted from some form of racial or religious prejudice than from any other cause. Our children will inherit the world we leave for them. Our choices today will shape that world. When we come to realize that we are all part of one very special team—humanity—we hold the key to learning to live together in peace.

Team spirit—genuine consideration for others—is the great hope for us all.

15

Secrets #13 and #14:

Poise   **Confidence**

I t was quite a sight! Twenty members of the Martin Marietta Total Quality Management (TQM) team standing hand in hand in a large circle trying frantically to pass two neon-colored hula hoops in opposite directions from one person to the next without letting go of one another! The hula hoop relay is a wonderful game of creativity, resourcefulness, and teamwork under time pressure. The players do everything they can to keep the hoops moving, twisting their bodies into all sorts of contortions. As the hoop approached each person it was great fun to watch the reaction. Some of the participants had huge grins on their faces. They couldn't wait to hop through those hoops! They were on their toes, revved up and raring to go. Others looked genuinely nervous. You could almost hear them asking themselves, "Will I be able to make it through without tripping or looking silly?"

As the instructor, I love the hula hoop relay. It is always one of the highlights of the Relay Paradigm seminar because it is a game absolutely loaded with surprise, wonderfully enabling principles of team synergy, and terrific fun. Today, the event was even more of an unexpected treat than usual. I always ask participants attending the Relay Paradigm seminar to wear casual, comfortable clothes. But today, some of the members of the TQM team had apparently not received the instructions about dress. Several were wearing full business attire. This was going to be a riot!

Keeping the Relay in Motion

One unsuspecting woman in particular faced a special challenge. Her formal, full-length crimson skirt was restrictive enough by itself, but when I noticed the four-inch high heels she wore on her feet, I knew we were sailing toward difficult seas! She smiled as she quietly waited for the game to begin, tightly gripping her teammates' hands. I was about to encourage her to remove her shoes when I spotted the playfulness in her eyes. I decided to keep quiet and see what would unfold.

In the hula hoop relay there are only two rules: Participants may not let go of one another's hands, and they are to act as a team. It is a game of speed. The goal of the game is for each of the two hoops to make one complete revolution around the circle in opposite directions, returning to where it began in the shortest possible time. The clock starts when I say "Go!" When both hoops are back to their original starting position the clock stops.

Up to this point in the seminar, the group had been a bit reserved. They were conscientious and attentive, but they had yet to let go and really play full out. The hula hoop relay has a way of breaking the ice and helping everyone remember how good it feels to be like a kid again.

Grace Under Pressure

As the hoops started moving around the circle, the energy in the room began to build. The participants tucked their heads as they twisted and turned, rushing to get through the hoops. Some were very graceful and smooth. Others were, well, *energetic.* When the hoop reached the woman in the long skirt, she hustled to step through as quickly as she could. Her head and shoulders slid through easily, but as she attempted to step over the bottom of the hoop, those treacherous four-inch heels caught in the lace fringe of her slip. The harder she tried to break free, the more tangled she became. I called out to her frantically, "It's snowing! It's snowing!" as I pointed to the slip that was now sliding down, down, down. But she absolutely refused to give up. She would not let go of her teammates' hands!

As she yanked her teammate down toward the ground, working to free the ensnarled slip from her heel with her left hand, she tried to hitch her slip back up by pulling it from the top with her right hand. Each time she instinctively pulled up on the back side of her skirt, her teammate on the "top side" turned a progressively brighter shade of red because she still kept a tight grip on his hand! All the while, she was completely determined to keep the hoop moving. It would have made a hilarious *I Love Lucy* episode!

At last, through sheer tenacity, she managed to free her slip from that deadly heel. The team let out a huge cheer, and the hoops finally completed their circuit. When I looked over at the woman, she was grinning from ear to ear. It was a smile not of embarrassment, but of pure fun. I am convinced that her smile, at that critical moment, was the primary catalyst for a remarkable team transformation that occurred throughout the rest of the seminar.

Without realizing it, the woman had given the team the perfect leadership they needed at that critical moment. The impact of her poise under pressure communicated far more clearly than words that what happens to us is much less important than how we handle life's happenings. This young woman had enabled her team to see that obstacles could actually be fun rather than fearsome. When the hoop became stuck, *she* didn't. She remained herself. She had decided that the hula hoop game was an opportunity to learn, to have fun, and to be completely present. She easily could have retreated into embarrassment or humiliation when things didn't go according to plan. Had she made that choice, our momentum would have come to a grinding halt. Instead, her poise released pressure and unleashed the team. This is the power of true poise.

Climb the Stairway of Self-Leadership

As we have discovered more secrets and moved higher through the Pyramid of Success we have seen that each succeeding stone has been built upon those below. The four outer stones along the left side of the pyramid form what I have come to call the Stairway of Self-Leadership.

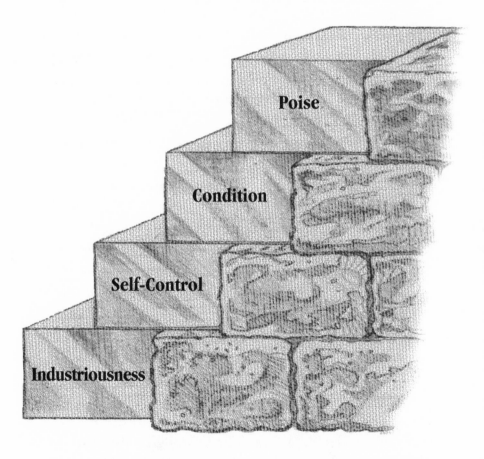

Self-leadership is the *internal* process of leadership. As we uncover the secrets of success on which the entire pyramid is based, we discover a simple yet profound truth: We cannot truly lead others until we learn to lead ourselves.

In chapter 2, I described the three-stage journey to internalize a vision. This is absolutely integral to successful self-leadership. You begin by *defining your vision*. One vision of self-leadership is to achieve genuine peace of mind, where you are fully resourceful regardless of the circumstances that surround you. The next step is to *live the vision*, gradually transforming the vision to your identity. This is a process of becoming that begins on the inside. Finally, as your vision becomes more and more the essence of who you are, you become a master of self-leadership. Masters of self-leadership communicate their vision not only through words and actions, but most profoundly through their *being*. The Stairway of Self-Leadership parallels this pathway, gradually ascending from effort to effortlessness.

The stairway begins with *industriousness*. We have learned that true industriousness is a function more of focus than of time. Industriousness is the result of being present and taking consistent actions to grow, to improve, and to contribute. When we apply concentration, energy, and heart to what we are actually doing in the present moment, we transform hard work into passion.

As we apply ourselves industriously to taking actions that lead toward our vision and our goals, we create results. *Self-control,* the second step in the stairway, becomes invaluable at this point. Through self-control, we begin to develop our ability to *accept* and *detach*. It is critical to recognize that results, in and of themselves, are neither good nor bad. We supply the meaning of any result. Acceptance is simply recognizing that results are neutral. Jim Rohn expressed this centerpiece of self-leadership beautifully when he said, "Nothing has any meaning except the meaning that we give to it!"

When we accept this simple truth about results, we enable ourselves to detach. Detachment does not mean we separate ourselves from the experience of an action or event. Instead, through self-control, we learn to detach ourselves from emotions that do not serve us. When we recognize that we supply the meaning of events, it becomes clear that the meaning we attach ignites our emotions. The meaning we give to events can paralyze us in fear, cut us off from hope, or fill us with rigidity and false pride.

When we apply concentration, energy, and heart to what we are actually doing in the present moment, we transform hard work into passion.

These feelings are based on the past, and we project them into the future. Thus, we take ourselves away from the only place where we can truly make a difference—the present moment. So, in a very real sense, when we detach from disabling feelings, we step out of the past and the future, and enter the present. By exercising our self-control and learning to accept and detach, we take a major step toward the ultimate goal of self-leadership, which is peace of mind.

We ascend to the next step in the Stairway of Self-Leadership when we consistently *condition* acceptance and detachment within ourselves. Through conditioning it becomes easier and easier to automatically exercise the self-control required to accept results as neutral and detach ourselves from emotions that direct us away from our true purpose. At this point we are deeply involved in living our vision and moving ever closer to transforming our vision to our identity.

How to Develop Poise

When we have conditioned self-control and industrious-ness into our subconscious, we ascend to the highest step in the Stairway of Self-Leadership. This step, *poise,* is not something you pursue; it is something you embody. True poise is simply being yourself. So many of us attempt to live multiple identities. We seem to be one person at work, another at home, and still another with friends or social groups. These multiple identities are driven by two destructive needs of the ego: the need for approval and the need to control others. These two needs are at the heart of every instance when we feel obsessed with hav-ing to be right. When we move beyond these needs, we find ourselves at ease in any situation. We stop fighting ourselves. This is the essence of poise.

Recently I attended a deeply moving seminar called The Master Key, led by an excellent teacher named Jim Britt. In the seminar, Jim described the person we become when we let go of the need for approval and the need to control others. This is the true self, the part of ourselves that is free from destructive ego.

We unleash our true selves first through noncritical self-observation, and second by developing the self-discipline to let go of the two destructive needs. For example, if you find yourself becoming incredibly angry and frustrated when you are caught in traffic, the first step to letting go is simply to observe your feelings. This is observation without assessment. Simple detachment often enables you to see that you are driving yourself batty out of a need to control a situation that is beyond your control. The next step is to ask yourself if you truly want to let go of the disempowering feelings now. Eventually, through repetition and conditioning, the self-observation and self-discipline become natural and automatic.

> **We unleash our true selves first through noncritical self-observation, and second by developing the self-discipline to let go of the two destructive needs.**

As leaders, the impact we create increases expo-
nentially when we pave the way for ourselves and our
teammates by letting go of the need for approval and the
need to control others. As we prepare for important
events, meetings, coaching sessions, and presentations,
we can create a very simple yet profoundly enabling ritual
by asking an important question of ourselves: Are the
actions I'm about to take aimed at either approval or control? If the answer is yes, take a deep and freeing breath,
and let the need go. Focus on what you can give rather
than what you can receive or demand. You will find yourself filled with poise and a magnetic calm, even in situations that seem to others to be extremely intense and
pressure-packed. Pressure comes only when we are driven by the need for approval or the need to control others. When we release this pressure, we are able to serve.
And, only when we are prepared to serve can we truly
lead.

Abandon the Need to Control Others

In *Leadership When the Heat's On,* Danny Cox writes of
the precipitous fall his sales team's performance took
from the very top to the very bottom of his company
when he tried to control and pressure them into
excellence.

> I had established a track record of expecting
> people to respond to me and my agenda
> without much, if any, regard for theirs. In
> the end, I got back what I gave out, which
> was not much empathy, tolerance, or under-

standing. The clone-maker had duplicated himself all right. All of the intolerance and lack of genuine concern I had demonstrated for my staff, they ended up demonstrating for me. I was about to exit this office as unceremoniously as I had allowed many of my top salespeople to do during my 'reign of terror.'

Later, Cox describes the dynamic change that took place in his team when he stopped trying to control them and strived, instead, to serve.

As it turned out, I didn't lose my job. Now that I think about it, I doubt that they could have found any sane person willing to take over that office after what I had done to it. More importantly, though, I jumped in with both feet, rolled up my sleeves, and resolved that I would be the best manager I could possibly be, which was an invitation, through more effective and genuine relationships, for all of my people to be the best that they could be. To my amazement, everyone in the organization responded and responded quickly. We began to give the appearance of and function like a team. I stopped demanding that they be me and began helping them be themselves. Four short months later, we were number one again.

When you exhibit genuine poise, others are drawn to you, both in business and in your personal life. You become a magnet. At a powerful subconscious level, people seem to know that you want them to feel free to be themselves. I experienced the remarkable power of poise to transform personal relationships when I met my wife, Carole.

Free Yourself from the Need for Approval

Throughout my years as a coach, I had focused so completely on my work that I had virtually no personal life. I pretended that this was the result of total dedication and simply being too busy for anything but coaching. In actuality, I was petrified of women! Inside, I deeply wanted to fall in love with the woman of my dreams. Even more, I wanted the woman of my dreams to fall in love with me. I looked for her in every woman I met. But I was so painfully shy and worried about making a good impression that I found it infinitely easier to avoid women altogether. On the few occasions I ventured out on dates, I felt so awkward and uncomfortable that the thought of another evening out was enough to cause me to schedule extra workouts!

Finally, in the summer after I left coaching, I began to understand that my fear arose from a deep and unsatisfied need for approval. When I was around women in social contexts outside of coaching, I felt like a different person. I had not yet accepted myself. I did not even know who I really was, outside of coaching.

That summer I decided to find out. I spent more quality time simply being present with myself than I had in the entire eight years of coaching. I moved to the great

Northwest and reveled in quiet moments in the woods and mountains. Daily exercise and running became a very special part of my life. As I ran, I allowed my mind to wander. I did not try to control my thoughts. It was a new experience for me. I was amazed at the creativity and peacefulness that emerged from within when I stopped trying to force every moment. I realized that running was one of the first genuine gifts I had ever given myself. I ran for the joy I felt, not to compete or to gain approval from anyone. It was a remarkably freeing new feeling!

I was just beginning my career in the transportation industry that summer. At work, I had almost endless energy and delighted in nearly every task that was thrown my way. After so many years of being in charge, it felt refreshing to immerse myself in learning about a new industry and environment. I found myself feeling surprisingly comfortable asking for help and saying "I don't understand" when an instruction or project didn't quite make sense to me. I learned quickly because I enjoyed the process of discovery. I began to see clearly how strong my need for approval and my need to control others had been during my later years in coaching. It was as if I had to be right—I had to know the answers—or I would somehow fail as a coach. I had desperately tried to be supercoach and, as a result, had stopped being myself. Now, in this summer of new awakening, I saw how limiting and stress-producing these choices had been. I had sought to be a great leader of others before I was a self-leader.

**I was amazed at the creativity
and peacefulness that
emerged from within when I
stopped trying to force every
moment.**

As I began to let go of these ego-driven needs, a wonderful new sense of balance came over me. With this new self-acceptance, I found that I was much more accepting of others as well. For the first time in my life, I felt at ease in situations I had previously avoided at all costs. I was amazed to find myself talking comfortably with women in social interactions both inside and outside the workplace. I developed real friendships with some terrific women. Instead of longing for their approval, I simply enjoyed them as human beings. This was new territory for me, and I loved it!

The Rewards of Self-Acceptance

Late that summer I was sent to Alaska on business. After a wonderful long run around Anchorage, I stopped in at the hotel spa to lift some weights and take a whirlpool bath. As I walked in, I noticed a sign offering hotel guests a special price on massages. I had never had a massage. Before that summer, I never would have taken the time to relax and indulge myself in something as luxuriating and quieting as a massage. I would have been too worried about what others would think. My ego-driven need for approval had infected every part of my life, even the choices I made about taking care of myself. But now, it seemed like an exciting new adventure. My muscles were tired from all my running and exercise. I thought it might be a great way to loosen up and release some soreness.

I didn't quite know what to expect as I entered the massage room. I could smell the wintergreen scent of the massage oil, and I felt a gentle peacefulness come over me as I lay on the table listening to soft instrumental music. When the massage therapist walked in I noticed how lovely she was. She smiled at me and introduced herself. "My name is Carole. I see this is the first time you've had a massage. Just relax and let go." Before this summer of self-acceptance and self-discovery, I would have been terrified at this point. But now, I felt genuinely comfortable with her. As she worked on my tired muscles we began to talk as if we were old friends. She was fascinating. I wanted to learn all about her. I was so at peace, I wasn't interested in trying to impress her. Instead, I simply wanted to share my thoughts and dreams, even my doubts and fears honestly with her. It was the first time I had ever experienced such a feeling of poise—truly being myself—in this kind of interaction with a woman.

The massage was wonderful and the conversation was even better. We had such a heartfelt connection right away that it seemed completely natural to ask her if she'd like to go to dinner with me. We had a wonderful evening together, talking until the wee hours of the morning. We have been together ever since.

We were married beside Lake Washington in Seattle a year later. We chose the autumn equinox for our wedding day, to symbolize the balance we had found through our love for one another. One of the vows I wrote to Carole that day expresses the joy, the peace, and the love that await us when poise replaces pursuit and we learn to truly accept ourselves. Though it was written in honor of finding my soul mate, the vow perfectly describes the process of discovering the self-leader within each of us.

Finding You

Before I knew you, I wondered where you were. I searched for you everywhere, hoping to find you in everyone I met. I couldn't find you. I began to wonder if you truly existed. Once, long ago, I wrote down a thought that could have shown me the way to you—if only I would have listened to my own words. "No one can be loved until they let themselves be seen. No one can be seen, until they learn to love themselves." Two years ago, I set out to find myself. When I finally began to like the person I had become, to truly accept myself, I began to think, to smile, and to talk. I stopped looking for you when I found myself—and there you were.

Reaching the Capstone on the Pyramid of Success

So, whatever your dreams of relationships or career, when you let go of ego and free your true self, you liberate the poise within you and ascend the Stairway of Self-Leadership. At the top of the stairway you will find that poise has joined with the fourteenth secret, the final stone in this fourth tier of the Pyramid of Success: *confidence.* If poise is simply being yourself, confidence is the inner knowledge that when you are yourself and others are free to be themselves, everything works out for the best.

The Leadership Triangle

In the Pyramid of Success, confidence rests above a smaller pyramid of its own. I call this substructure the Leadership Triangle, for it represents the foundational truth on which great leadership of others ultimately depends: You cannot be a great leader unless your confidence in others is as strong as your confidence in yourself. For example, how effective would a teacher be who possessed great confidence in his ability to teach, but little confidence in his students' ability to learn? Each of the qualities in the Leadership Triangle involves our relationships with others. These qualities are connected by unyielding belief in the human spirit. As a leader your belief or lack of belief in others shines through. Others sense when your confidence is confined to yourself. To bring out the best in others and yourself, you must steadfastly believe that there is greatness in everyone.

The foundation of the Leadership Triangle consists of friendship, loyalty, cooperation, and enthusiasm. These are the seeds of true confidence. We must feel great joy in connecting with others and combining our talents and energies if we are to become leaders who exude and stimulate genuine confidence.

You cannot be a great leader unless your confidence in others is as strong as your confidence in yourself.

The next row in the Leadership Triangle focuses on preparation. We must have faith that we have prepared ourselves and our team for virtually any challenge if the seeds of confidence are to take root and begin to sprout. In a garden, it is not enough merely to plant seeds and expect a bountiful harvest. We must carefully observe the new growth and take necessary actions such as weeding, watering, and enriching the soil. In cultivating our confidence as leaders, *alertness, initiative,* and *intentness* are essential qualities if we are to be fully prepared to bring out our best. By being alert, we position ourselves to seize moments of opportunity to take action, to acknowledge, and to learn. We trigger our Reticular Activating System to focus clearly on what we want, not what we don't want. Fed with information we receive from being alert, we use our initiative to become proactive decision makers. Each time we exercise our initiative, we receive valuable feedback to help us determine if we are moving in the direction of our true intent.

Guided by our intent and constantly improving through the combination of alertness and initiative, we deepen our confidence in ourselves and others by merging the five master skills of winning leadership with an eager *team spirit.* Each of the five master skills—
- flexibility
- enabling questioning
- visualization
- letting go
- expressing yourself with dimension

—is enhanced when we apply it unselfishly to the development of others. As our skill grows and our team spirit deepens, we gain both the knowledge and inspiration required to let our confidence fully blossom. We reach the apex of the Leadership Triangle when we feel supreme confidence in ourselves, in our team, and in what we accomplish together.

That level of confidence leaves an indelible stamp on everyone around you. They feel tremendously grateful to be a part of your team. Your confidence provides a profound sense of clarity about what is truly important. Such certainty about priorities relieves stress and sets you and your team directly on purpose.

A Shining Example of Confidence

There is no better model of unwavering confidence than Coach Wooden. He remains extremely modest and humble about his accomplishments because he gives credit for these achievements to his players and, above all, to God. His confidence is quiet and steady because it is based not on outcomes, but rather on the concentration and energy he puts into preparation.

Coach Wooden never concerned himself with pursuing perfection. Instead, he focused on effort and continuous improvement. Consequently, he was neither devastated by losses nor overexcited by wins. He spoke often to his players about the importance of consistent confidence, as opposed to dependence on emotional peaks, to perform at the team's best. For every peak, he believed, there was a corresponding valley. As the swiftest, most direct route to reaching the team's potential, he advocated calm assurance in the players and their preparation, combined with an insatiable desire to improve. His teams reflected this philosophy and absorbed his unfailing confidence into their own hearts.